LIFE IN THE SPIRIT FOR YOUR KIDS

Life in the Spirit for Your Kids

Ken Wilson
and
Dave Mangan

DK Publications
Ann Arbor, Michigan

DK Publications
3235 Edgewood Drive
Ann Arbor. Michigan 48104

Cover design by David Mangan

93 94 10 9 8 7 6 5 4 3 2

Printed in the United States of America
ISBN 0-89283-639-3

Library of Congress-in Publication Data

Wilson. Ken, 1952-
   Life in the Spirit for Your Kids / Ken Wilson and David Mangan.
     p.   cm.
    ISBN 0-89283-639-3
    1. Church work with youth.   2. Youth—Religious life.
3.   Baptism in the Holy Spirit.   4. Youth—Prayerbooks and
4.   devotions—English.   I. Mangan, David, 1944-   II. Title
BV4447.W57 1990
268'.432—dc20   90-37976
                                    CIP

Contents

Testimonies

PART ONE

Children of the Promise:
For Those Concerned to Pass on the Life of Jesus Christ to a New Generation

"The promise is for you and your children."

Acts 2:39

ONE

A Chosen Generation

"**K**EN AND NANCY, sometime in the next three days, you're going to lose this baby. I'm sorry to tell you that, but you will need to be ready."

We listened in stunned silence to the doctor's prediction. Nancy was five months pregnant. She had been admitted to the hospital with severe uterine cramping and bleeding. We were too young to be parents—just out of high school. This pregnancy was a "crisis pregnancy." Abortion had been suggested as an alternative, yet even though we were not Christians at the time, we couldn't tolerate the thought. So we got married and began the great adventure.

But the obstetrician's words helped us to realize even more clearly that we wanted this child to live. That night a friend visited us in the hospital. Without a word to us, he went home and asked all of his Christian friends to pray for the baby and for us. That night, to the doctor's surprise the bleeding slowed dramatically and later stopped.

When our son was born on the second day of 1970, I wanted to avoid a biblical name. Names like Joshua seemed to be the rage and I wanted none of it. So we named him Jesse, after the Olympian, Jesse Owens. My father informed us that Jesse was indeed a biblical name: Jesse was the father of King David.

In less than six months, Nancy and I had given our lives to Christ. Our friend eventually told us about the prayers that night when Nancy was bleeding in the hospital. Browsing through one of those "Name Your Baby" books in the grocery store, I looked up the meaning of our newborn son's name. Jesse means "God exists."

The births of many children in this generation have born powerful witness to the kingdom of God. My friend Paul was far off from God. His mother, a believer, decided to pray that her unborn grandchild would have a Christian father. Paul, of course, shrugged this off as another example of his mother's religious sentimentalism.

In the delivery room, Paul saw the crowning head of the baby and his mind flashed back to his experimentation with illegal drugs. He was sure that she would be grossly deformed. Moments later, when his beautiful daughter was born breathing, kicking, and crying, Paul's heart melted. Then and there, he surrendered his life to Jesus. Arista had a Christian father.

Is the present generation—newborns to young adults—a generation specially chosen, set apart for the purposes of God? I believe it is.

In the early seventies, a group of young parents and youth workers from our fellowship gathered to pray for the beginning of our "youth ministry." Very quickly we were flooded with a conviction that the light of the generation to come—our young children—would far outshine our light. At the time, we were at the crest of a wave of renewal and revival; our prayer meetings had doubled in size from three hundred fifty to seven hundred in a single year. College students were awakening to the gospel in droves. People from around the world, including influential church leaders, were visiting us to see what God was doing. Frankly, we thought *our* generation was pretty hot stuff. Yet the message that we took to be from the Holy Spirit was insistent, "The light they bear will far outshine your own."

Nearly twenty years later, we can see that there is indeed an unprecedented level of spiritual warfare surrounding this generation of young people. In the Scriptures, whenever a generation was specially chosen to witness a new in-breaking of the kingdom of heaven, that generation was also marked for extraordinary spiritual attack.

For example, the generation of Moses was chosen as the generation to witness a great deliverance from four hundred years of bondage in Egypt—a deliverance that would gain the people of Israel and her God great reknown. Was it mere coincidence that Pharaoh decreed that all the male babies born to Israelite women should be killed—a mass, state-sanctioned infanticide?

Similarly, the generation of Jesus was chosen to witness the resurrection of Jesus, the outpouring of the Holy Spirit, and the birth of the New Covenant church. These events are still sending shock waves through every culture exposed to the gospel. Was it mere coincidence that King Herod ordered the execution of boys under the age of two years in that region? Perhaps some of the original apostles and eyewitnesses to Jesus were at risk, along with Christ.

This present generation of young people finds itself in a unique position to spread the gospel, with the unprecedented possibility of a truly worldwide evangelistic explosion. Prophetic voices from many different streams are saying that a time of great harvest for the kingdom of God is at hand. Is it mere coincidence that in 1973, the United States Supreme Court legalized abortion on demand, which in subsequent years has eliminated fully a third of the generation now in school? Think of it: a third of your children's would-be classmates never made it to school because of abortion.

Whenever God decides to move in great power with a particular generation, the powers of darkness unleash an unholy tide of death. Surely such a tide is seeking to overtake our children. In 1950, the top three discipline problems in secondary schools were talking, making noise, and gum chewing. Thirty years later the top three problems are drug and alcohol abuse, pregnancy, and suicide.

Often the effect of these sobering statistics is to rob parents of hope. How can we stand against this cultural tide? Who will be left standing to receive the baton of faith when our leg of the relay is done and the next generation's is due?

But the fact is, life triumphs over death in Jesus Christ. The generation of Moses was marked for slaughter, but Moses and Aaron and Miriam and others who took part in the Exodus survived to see the salvation of the God of Israel. The generation of Christ was the target of an organized infanticide, yet Jesus himself was spared, along with a generation who became witnesses to his resurrection and ambassadors of his message to the known world.

God has a sovereign purpose for this generation which no demonic counter-purpose will ultimately be allowed to thwart. In Belfast, Northern Ireland, an interdenominational group of Catholics and Protestants sing a song with the refrain, "This is the generation of those who seek the Lord; this is the generation called to prepare his way." The son I referred to at the beginning of this chapter recently spent a year in Belfast, studying at Queen's University with two of his friends, Chris and Joe. During their first week in town, a priest with a ministry of evangelism asked the young men to accompany him to fourteen high schools in West Belfast and invite all who were interested to a series of evangelistic evening meetings.

The young American men caught the attention of the tough high school assemblies with a disarming "Bible Rap" song. Four hundred young people came to the first evening session. The crowd looked skeptical—standing with their arms folded, smoking in the lobby, hanging out with their dates. But the singing, simple testimonies from people their age, and preaching of the gospel had an effect. They came back night after night.

At the last session, seven hundred young people filled the church. The priest invited the Holy Spirit to fall on the crowd of teenagers, many from rough backgrounds, some with close connections to the Irish Republican Army. The power of God descended on the whole group. The pews were soon full of Irish young people sobbing, laughing with new joy, repenting of their sins, giving their lives to Jesus.

"This is the generation of those who seek the Lord; this is the generation called to prepare his way." God is preparing to unleash a wave of the Holy Spirit that will rescue this generation and transform them. They will become rescuers who will call their peers to repentance and bring them the love of Christ.

Your children and the young people you know are destined to be part of something very big. God is not withholding himself from them, but is prepared to draw near and reveal himself in Jesus Christ.

This book can help you present the gospel of Jesus to members of this chosen generation so that they can personally respond to him. We have found that the children and young people who hear this message do believe, receive, and respond to Jesus. We present it with the prayer that the young people you know and love will hear the call of Christ to them and emerge as a generation destined to bear a great light to the world.

TWO

The Holy Spirit
in My Living Room

IN 1967 I HAD A SURPRISING ENCOUNTER WITH GOD near Duquesne University, outside of Pittsburgh, Pennsylvania. I was on a retreat weekend with an assortment of students. We were not an impressive bunch spiritually. Many of us were at our wits end with life, struggling, groping, barely surviving. We were confused about the meaning of the Christian faith. Some of us were seriously confused.

It was late afternoon when I walked into the retreat center chapel. Suddenly, I was experiencing something I had never known before—the extraordinary presence of God. God's love came over me. I mean really came over me. I laughed, I cried, and fell facedown on the floor—overwhelmed by this love.

Then I did something that surprised me even more. I began to pray in a language I did not know. Before long, I wasn't the only one. Whatever I was experiencing was touching some of the others as well.

I didn't know what to think at the time, or how to describe what was happening. Later, I realized that I was being touched by the Holy Spirit, what others later would call being "baptized" or "filled" with the Holy Spirit.

At the time, David Mangan, the young man in the chapel, had no idea that this experience would be described as the beginning of the charismatic renewal in the Catholic church. This work of the Holy Spirit, which has touched the lives of millions of Roman Catholics, is just one wave among many that has stirred the churches—Catholic, Protestant, and Orthodox—since the dawn of the twentieth century. The Pentecostal movement, the Neo-Pentecostal movement, the Jesus People movement, the charismatic renewal in mainline churches, and more recently the rediscovery of signs and wonders among evangelicals and fundamentalists, are all part of an unprecedented outpouring of the Holy Spirit.

Over the next twenty years, David and his wife, Barbara, had five children: Erica, Aimee, Shawna, David, and Ann. David and Barb's lives had been deeply influenced by this outpouring of the Spirit. But they wondered if their children could experience the Spirit's action in the same way.

They decided to try something. They presented what was called a "Life in the Spirit Seminar" to their oldest daughter and two of her friends. After observing the good fruit from this experience, they decided to present the seminar to their four oldest children whose ages ranged from five to eleven. (Their eldest daughter went through it again with her brother and sisters.)

The Life in the Spirit Seminar, a series of seven talks, had been developed by Ralph Martin and other leaders in the early days of the charismatic renewal. It had been used throughout the world to bring thousands, perhaps millions of adults to a deeper personal conversion to Christ and a release of the Holy Spirit, often referred to as being "baptized in the Spirit."

David had conducted Life in the Spirit Seminars many times, praying with countless adults to be filled with the Spirit. But he had never done this with children. Certainly not his own children. Not in his own living room.

The Mangans had spoken to their children of God's love often. They attended church and prayer meetings with them. They prayed together as a family. But they didn't know what to expect from the children. Would they respond or would this pass over their heads?

In Acts 2:39, it is recorded that the promise of Pentecost "is for you and your children." Was it really possible for them to know what John Wesley referred to as the "internal witness" of the Spirit's presence? Could they receive power from God to live the life of Christ—power to pray, to worship, to hear the voice of God, in their own way to serve him? They didn't know, but thought it was worth a try.

As you can imagine, David adapted the talks substantially. He shortened the series to five weeks and simplified the content. He also included a presentation of "The Four Spiritual Laws" developed by Campus Crusade for Christ.

A high-school math teacher, Dave was no expert in the religious education of children. But he knew enough to keep it short, keep it simple, and make it concrete wherever possible. For the most part, the children listened, understood the basic points, and even asked some very good questions. They seemed to look forward to the sessions.

Then the day arrived to pray with the children to explicitly receive Christ as Savior and Lord and be filled with the Spirit. David and Barbara were amazed at how quickly and easily the children responded. One by one they went to each child, led them in a prayer of repentance and com-

mitment, then laid hands on them to receive the gift of the
Spirit. They had told the children about the gift of tongues
and as they asked, each child began to quietly speak in
tongues.

Apparently the whole experience made quite an impression on young David, who was in kindergarten at the time. A
few days after the prayer session, he was playing with his
sister Ann, who at the age of two didn't participate in the
talks and prayer session with the rest of the family. Out of
sight of her two youngest children, Barbara observed a
remarkable exchange.

David was telling his sister about the love of God and
what a good thing it was to "ask Jesus into your heart." Ann
was listening intently. Her brother then positioned two
small chairs facing each other, and they sat down. He took
her hands and asked, "Do you want to receive Jesus into
your heart now?"

Ann nodded.

David led her in a simple prayer, instructing her to pray
after him. Then he asked her whether she wanted to receive
the Holy Spirit.

Again, Ann nodded.

The young evangelist prayed again and suggested his
sister pray in tongues, which he proceeded to do. Ann
followed suit.

Later that day, Barbara asked her husband, "Could that
have been real?" He responded, "I don't know ... but why
not?" Why not, indeed?

 Since that time David and others have prayed with
hundreds of children to give their lives to Jesus and be
baptized in the Spirit. Usually, they are older than Ann,
fourth to ninth graders being the most common age group.
God always responds to them. If they ask to be filled with

the Spirit, they are. Incidentally, if they ask to speak in tongues, they do.

Of course, that doesn't mean that all of these children go on to live committed Christian lives. But neither do adults who experience the same things. The point is, God is willing to come to children in these ways—as he does with adults but according to their age and maturity. And children respond to God.

Young people (including very young children) can be filled with the Holy Spirit. They can praise God expressively. They can receive and exercise charismatic gifts of the Spirit. Of course, this doesn't make them into mini-spiritual dynamos. They are still, after all, children or young adults. They are still on the way, under construction, immature.

Their experience of God ebbs and flows. They have times of noticeable spiritual growth as well as times of relative dormancy. Being filled with the Spirit can be for them a momentary spiritual high, or it can be part of a process that moves them into full Christian maturity. The life of the Spirit can be quenched—by personal choice, by the influence of the world, and other factors—or it can be nurtured. Simply stated, they are a lot like adults.

THREE

How to Use This Book

THIS BOOK IS INTENDED AS A RESOURCE for anyone who wants to help young people live for Christ. Naturally, the first question that comes to mind is, what do you mean by "young people," kindergarteners or high-school students?

We've attempted to aim the presentations, examples, and so on to cover an age span from early readers to early teens. You can read the chapters in the next section—designed to be read by or with young people—and judge for yourself whether they hit the mark for those you have in mind.

We have had occasion to present this material to a group of fourth through ninth graders—a fairly wide age span. In doing so, we found it most effective to aim the presentations toward the older end of the spectrum. Nothing is more deadly to communication with young people than to have them feel that you are speaking down to them. So we've tried to make the presentations lively enough—with illustrations, simple points, and so on—to speak to young minds without adopting a "kiddie tone" that would lose the older ages. By adopting this straightforward tone, the younger ages realize that the issues we are considering are important ones.

PURPOSE

The purpose of the book is threefold.

1. To present the basic message of Jesus and lead children to an explicit response. Often children are exposed to the Christian message in a Christian home, but never have the opportunity to respond personally and accept that message in an explicit way—to say "yes" to Jesus. Through the use of this book, they can have such an opportunity.

Naturally, this raises an important question. What does it mean for a child to make a personal commitment to Christ? Surely the "yes" of a ten-year-old is different than the "yes" of a young adult, which in turn is different than the commitment of someone who is forty years old. It is true that a child's will or capacity to choose is not fully developed. Nonetheless children can exercise their developing capacity to choose, and Scripture records examples of significant choices made by children.

Samuel was a boy when God spoke to him and called him to serve as a prophet, to dedicate himself to God. Samuel heard the Lord, and responded to God's call.

Many biblical scholars believe that Mary, the mother of Jesus, may have been as young as thirteen when the angel announced God's plan to bring the Messiah into the world through her. She was able to say, "Yes, Lord. Let it be done to me according to your will." And her yes counted.

Especially in cultures like our own, which have been largely secularized, children of Christian families are called to be different than their peers. They won't watch the same television programs or listen to the same music. In some respects, they will behave and think differently than other children. These children will be marching to the beat of a different drummer.

In such a setting, it is even more important for Christian children to make an explicit identification with the Lord, to say, "Yes, I am a Christian; I want to follow Jesus and live the way he wants me to live." The choice of an eight-year-old may be immature, but it is valid. And it can pave the way for more significant choices and steps of personal commitment to the Lord later in life.

2. To bring children into personal contact with the power of the Holy Spirit. The terms used to describe this may vary. And Christians of various theological convictions may prefer one term to another, or understand them differently. One thing is certain, the promise of the Holy Spirit is available to children. And the unique role of the Holy Spirit is to make the new life of Christ a living reality in every believer. The Holy Spirit communicates, imparts, and applies to each of us the life of God.

At times we will speak of this reality—the impartation of the gift of the Spirit—as being baptized in the Holy Spirit, or being filled with the Holy Spirit. It is not necessary to view this as a single definitive work of the Holy Spirit—what a classical Pentecostal might refer to as the "Baptism in the Spirit" or the "Second Blessing," an action of God subsequent to and clearly distinct from basic conversion. In fact the theological convictions of the authors (Protestant Evangelical and Roman Catholic) would view the impartation of the Spirit, especially in the life of a child growing up in a Christian home as an unfolding process—marked, perhaps, by watershed events—but a process nonetheless.

Again, what does it mean for a child to be baptized in the Holy Spirit or filled with the Holy Spirit, or to use another term, experience a release of the Holy Spirit?

My daughter Amy was ten years old when we attended a six-week series based on the material in this book. David

Mangan led the sessions which consisted of about fifty fourth through ninth graders, along with their parents. When we prayed with Amy to be baptized or filled with the Holy Spirit, she began to quietly pray in tongues.

During the six weekly sessions she was encouraged to take a short period of time each day to pray and read the daily meditations provided. Since that time Amy has been taking a personal time for daily prayer. During this time she reads from her Bible and prays for a few minutes. I was surprised by her new-found motivation to pray. When I asked her recently if she has sensed the Lord saying anything to her personally, Amy replied, "He's been reminding me to pray every day."

On another occasion, we were talking at the dinner table about spiritual warfare. Amy rather shyly volunteered that some weeks previously she had sensed the Lord telling her that there was a spiritual attack being launched against our church. She sensed that as she was walking to a particular friend's house. Amy decided to pray for protection for the church whenever she walked this particular route.

Keep in mind my daughter, now eleven, is still a young fifth-grade girl. She argues with her sister and does all the other things normal for a girl her age. Now and then, she has been "led" to go off to her room to pray when it's her turn for dishes, and has needed my help to discern that the inspiration can wait until the dishes are washed!

This was not Amy's first experience of the Spirit's presence in her life. She wasn't a pagan before attending the weekly sessions and a newborn Christian afterwards. But the experience of explicitly committing her life to Christ in the presence of others (especially some peers!), being prayed with, and receiving a release of the Spirit was an important step for her.

As Amy matures, I expect she will have other significant times when she will be filled again with the Spirit, experiences that will correspond with new maturity. And she will likely face obstacles and challenges to her faith. In the meantime, she is being strengthened by the Spirit to live as a Christian today.

Throughout the book, we've included brief accounts from young people describing the action of God in their lives. Their stories give some inkling about what is possible for young people.

3. A third aim is to help young people to talk about the issues of a personal relationship with God in Christ. Many parents and others who work with young people find that speaking with young people about knowing God, receiving his love, and responding to his Spirit is surprisingly awkward. If they have had discussions of this kind, it has almost always been with other adults, using adult language, concerning adult issues. But when it comes to helping their own children understand and personally respond to the good news of Christ, they are at a loss. It's like talking with your kids about sex—a great idea, but how do you get started?

The material in this book provides an opportunity for parents and children to begin talking together about these issues. It gives the young people a chance to ask questions, an opportunity for parents and others to share their own stories of coming to know the love of God in Christ, and time to ask the young folks what they think about certain issues. Have they noticed that something seems to be very wrong with the world? Can they identify something inside themselves that prompts them to sin?

VARIOUS WAYS TO USE THE BOOK

The second section of the book consists of six chapters written for young people, covering the central issues of knowing God through his Son, Jesus Christ.

Parents or other leaders can read the chapters with the young persons, or use these chapters as a guide and resource for their own presentation. The latter option allows for adjusting the material to the particular needs of the person or group, but it also takes more nerve, time, and preparation.

Chapter five, "Draw Near" provides the opportunity for the young person to make a personal commitment to Jesus and be prayed with to receive a release of the Holy Spirit. It is the *action* chapter, both for the parents and the young person.

If you are like most parents, you may feel a bit nervous about chapter five. How do I do it? Will it work? What if nothing happens? Don't worry. It is simple. Jesus is the one who draws young people to the Father and fills them with the Spirit. You couldn't do it if you tried. But you can ask with the young person and you can pray with the young person.

Because the idea is new to many people (not because it is difficult!), we will devote a whole chapter to leading the dedication session. Hopefully by then you will see how simple it is and how little it depends on you.

DAILY MEDITATIONS

After the six chapters written for the young people, you will find a Daily Meditations section. These twenty-five meditations are written for young people. The daily meditations correspond to the content of the chapters: the first five meditations are on the theme of chapter one, "God's Love," the second five meditations on the theme of chapter two, "What's Wrong?" and so on. There are no meditations after the last chapter. If you decide to read one chapter per week, the meditations can be used during the week to reinforce the main points. If you prefer to read the chapters at a different pace, the meditations can be used after the book is completed.

Parents can read the meditations with their children each day, or the young person may prefer to set aside a few minutes to read them by himself or herself. The period of time just before bed—once all the bedtime preparations are over—is an especially good time for this. Naturally, deferring "lights out" for any length of time to use the meditations will drastically increase motivation! As you can imagine, the meditations can also be a springboard for a daily devotional time for the young person.

You will notice that after the meditations, there are four testimonies written by young people. You can choose one of these per week to read to your children. These stories will serve to encourage them. Although they are at the end of the book they are not meant to be read last. Rather they should serve to heighten your children's anticipation of what God can do for them over the course of the following weeks.

SETTING

This book has been designed for use in a variety of settings. It can be used by parents with their own children at home—either one-on-one or with the whole family. The

Mangan family has used this material together as a family in each of the past few years as a Lenten observance.

The book can be used within the context of a Sunday school class or some other church-sponsored instruction. It can be used as a preparation for confirmation in some church traditions, or as a preparation for baptism within churches that baptize older children. We've attempted to write from the common core of Christian truth—that which is shared by all the Christian churches—as summarized, for example, in the Apostles' and Nicene Creeds. You may wish to adapt or add material to reflect a distinctive teaching or emphasis from your theological tradition. It can be given within a youth ministry, or within a Christian school to a large number of children.

In our day, the Spirit wants to "turn the hearts of the fathers to their children, and the hearts of the children to their fathers" (Malachi 4:6). If the material is to be used in a group setting, consider including the mothers or fathers of the young people as an integral part of the program whenever possible. Parents can attend the sessions, discuss the content with their children, and participate in praying with them during the time of dedication.

FORMAT

We recommend a weekly format, that is, covering one chapter each week for six weeks. Under this format, the daily meditations can be used after each chapter (except the final chapter) to regularly reinforce the material.

Select a regular time and place, one that is likely to support the young person's attention and participation.

Finding a time when there is no serious competition for the child's time is important. If the kids are accustomed to rushing home from school for a snack and some free play— another time is advised! Don't plan to compete with a young person's favorite television program (of course you know all that).

We have found an evening time to be ideal, especially if homework can be avoided or handled earlier in the day. (Saturday evening minimizes the homework problem.) If younger children can to stay up later than their normal bedtime, this can provide a noticeable incentive for participation.

For home use, consider what you might do to make the time attractive and special. For example, you could save a popular meal or dessert for this particular night, so that everyone is looking forward to the evening. Or decide to celebrate the completion of the book with a special outing. . . . You get the picture.

Find a physical environment that minimizes distraction. If you're at home, perhaps you could unplug the phone. A place that allows everyone to be comfortable and relaxed (but not to lie down or fall asleep!) is best. Using the same setting each week can build a sense of continuity. Remember that kids are concrete creatures, and the physical setting can communicate much to them.

The level of spontaneity and formality will vary depending on many factors. If the book is used in a larger group setting the following format could be used:

- **Gathering Together**
  Start with a few words of introduction/reminder.
  "This is our first session to consider Life in the Spirit

which will last for six weeks. We're here to learn about God and to take some steps toward knowing him better and being filled with his Holy Spirit."

- **Brief Opening Prayer**
  This is a time to begin to introduce various forms of prayer and worship: singing, praying aloud together, vocal praise, prayers of thanksgiving, praying set prayers together, hand clapping. It can be a time to teach and practice various prayer postures: standing, lifting hands, bowing, kneeling. Add a little bit to your groups' "prayer repertoire" each week.

- **Presentation**
  Each chapter can be read in ten to fifteen minutes. During the reading (or presentation based on the chapter), involve the participants in some active way. Solicit answers to questions posed in the presentation. Take a few moments aside to say a brief Scripture passage together, or to repeat a key point aloud together.

  Depending on the size of the group, you may want to encourage and entertain questions during the presentation.

- **Brief closing together**
  Close with a song of praise or a prayer related to the topic, etc. Include a reminder to use the daily meditations between sessions.

- **Refreshments**

One final word of caution! If you are planning to use this book in your home with one or two of your children, do not—repeat, do not—be intimidated by all this group format business! The informality and flexibility of the home can be very effective. For example, you may feel that your son or daughter isn't receptive on a particular day. So you wait for a better time. You know your own children better than anyone else. You will know best how to use this book!

FOUR

How Does God Relate to Kids?

H OW DOES GOD RELATE TO CHILDREN? Think about your own experience as a child. Chances are, God was more involved than your first impressions might suggest.

My mother was an Episcopalian who attended church regularly. My father was an agnostic, who supported my mother in her church commitment, but did not share her faith.

As a boy, I can remember times when Christianity meant very little to me. Church was boring and sometimes downright unpleasant, especially when we had to kneel "forever," or so it seemed. But there were other times when God seemed very real.

I vividly remember going to the basement as a ten-year-old and telling God that it was fine with me if he wanted to take my grandmother home to be with him. She was having another heart attack upstairs and it seemed like the best thing. When she died later that day, I felt sure she was in God's hands.

I can remember the story of my other grandmother's death (which I had a special interest in since it occurred in my bedroom!). Apparently, "Gammy" as we called her—a Victorian Episcopalian Englishwoman—saw angels in my closet just before she died.

Through most of my childhood, I prayed the Lord's Prayer before going to sleep at night. No one told me to do that. I just did each night, usually very quickly. I also asked God to bless my family, my friends, and everyone else in the world, just so no one would feel left out.

As an older child I developed serious doubts about God. During my confirmation class, I learned that human beings were created for the glory of God. I learned that God wanted human beings to praise him. For some reason, this angered me. I thought God was an egomaniac.

A few years after my confirmation, I stopped attending church. In fact, I disavowed any relationship with God— telling him in no uncertain terms that if he existed, I didn't need him. For several years I thought little of God. I attended the church youth group for a brief time, in the hopes of getting to know a particular girl better. But I wouldn't call this the return of the prodigal son. Later, in my first year of college, I was drawn to examine the claims of Jesus and eventually dedicated my life to him.

At the time, I viewed myself as a pagan who had converted and become a Christian. In many respects, this was accurate. But looking back with a little more objectivity, I can see that my knowledge of God did not begin when I prayed the sinner's prayer. God was involved in my life from early childhood. And I was, in various ways, responding to him.

How does God relate to children? To answer this question, we can begin with the biblical evidence.

1. First of all, the New Testament views the children of believers as *holy*. In Paul's first letter to the Corinthians, he answered some questions about divorce. Should a believing wife divorce her unbelieving husband if he is willing to live with her? Paul answered no.

> For the unbelieving husband has been sanctified through his wife, and the unbelieving wife has been sanctified through her believing husband. Otherwise, your children would be unclean, but as it is, they are holy. 1 Corinthians 7:14

Apparently, the questioner thought that the unbelieving partner might in some way defile the Christian by association. Paul indicated that, on the contrary, the unbelieving partner shared in a kind of sanctification (not saving faith) by association with the Christian. As supporting evidence, Paul pointed to the fact that the children of a believer married to an unbeliever were holy.

While the reasoning may seem foreign to our non-Jewish (for those of us who are not Jewish) ears, the principle established is important. The children of believers are holy.

The root meaning of the word "holy" is "set apart for God" or "belonging to God." Children born to a Christian mother or father, in a particular way, belong to God. This follows from the fact that the entirety of every Christian's life belongs to God—time, money, resources, the future—everything including the believer's family and his or her children. God claims it all as his own.

Different church traditions have different ways of expressing this. In many churches infants are baptized. In others, baptism is deferred to a later time and children are "dedicated to the Lord." But virtually every church recognizes that the children of believers belong to God.

Of course this means that parents, while assuming responsibility to raise their children, do not "own" their children. If you are a Christian parent, your children don't, in a certain sense, belong to you. They belong to God.

God has a prior and absolute claim over your children. You may have certain hopes and dreams for your children. You may have plans that you wish them to fulfill. They may be good hopes, good dreams, good plans. But you have to bow before God's prior claim over your children. His plans may be different than your own.

2. Second, there is ample evidence in the Scripture of God's desire to establish intimacy with children. In the Old Testament, Samuel was a young boy serving as an assistant in the Temple. God spoke to him in an audible voice, calling his name. Samuel didn't know who was speaking to him at first. But with some help from Eli, he realized that it was God, and he answered God's voice. And the Lord called Samuel to serve him as a prophet.

In the New Testament, Jesus insisted on relating to young children.

> People were bringing little children to Jesus to have him touch them, but the disciples rebuked them. When Jesus saw this, he was indignant. He said to them, "Let the little children come to me, and do not hinder them, for the kingdom of God belongs to such as these. . . ." And he took the children in his arms, put his hands on them and blessed them. Mark 10:13-14, 16

These are strong words. The kingdom of God belongs to little children as well as adults. Let the little children come to Jesus. Don't keep them away from him. Don't hinder them.

In the New Testament epistles, children are specifically addressed along with others in the Christian community: "Children, obey your parents in everything, for this pleases the Lord" (Colossians 3:20).

Paul doesn't simply tell the parents to secure obedience. He speaks directly to the children, reasoning with them, appealing to their own interest in pleasing the Lord. This clearly presumes that the children were responsive to an appeal of this kind.

3. The Scripture speaks of salvation as a process as well as an event. For those of us who had little meaningful experience as Christian children, who were converted as adults, it is easy to focus on the event aspect of salvation: "One evening in May 1971 I gave my life to Christ," or "I was baptized seven years ago, and became a child of God."

In fact, in every Christian's life, there are important "salvation events." Some, like baptism, are definitive events—clear lines that are crossed—events with a "before and after" dimension.

But salvation is also a process. We are saved, and yet we are being saved. None of us is finished being saved yet.

We know that the whole creation has been groaning as in the pains of childbirth right up to the present time. Not only so, but we ourselves, who have the firstfruits of the Spirit, groan inwardly as we eagerly wait for our adoption as sons, the redemption of our bodies. For in this hope we were saved. But hope that is seen is no hope at all. Who hopes for what he already has? But if we hope for what we do not yet have, we wait for it patiently. **Romans 8:22-25**

If we think of salvation as a process, punctuated by specific events which can have a significant impact in a child's relationship with God, we have a framework to understand how a child enters into the Christian experience.

Some of the events are tied to important church initiation

rites: baptism in water, infant dedication, confirmation, a young person's first communion, and a public confession of faith are examples of these rites in various church traditions.

But there are also events which are less formal, more individualized, more personalized—perhaps some life experience that makes the reality of the Christian faith more clear. For many children (and this was the case for me as a child), the death of a close family member or friend can be such an event. A young child may "pray to receive Jesus into his heart," make a step of faith in a Christian camp setting or any number of other memorable events which move him or her along in the salvation process.

Children may feel insecure about whether they are going to heaven or hell, and find reassurance through a work of the Spirit in them.

They may experience some obviously divine protection— a close brush with death, an auto accident where they are spared from what might have been serious injury. The possibilities are as endless as the variety of experiences that children can have, all of which work together to draw them into a deeper knowledge of God.

4. The kingdom comes to children progressively. Jesus underscored the progressive nature of the kingdom in a series of short parables.

> This is what the kingdom of God is like. A man scatters seed on the ground. . . . All by itself the soil produces grain—first the stalk, then the head, then the full kernel in the head.

> What shall we say the kingdom of God is like?. . . It is like a mustard seed, which is the smallest seed you plant in the ground. Yet when planted, it grows and becomes the

largest of all garden plants, with such big branches that the birds of the air can perch in its shade. Mark 4:26, 28; 30-32

In thinking of a child's relationship to God, it is important to remember that the kingdom of God comes progressively—in stages, over time.

Some of the growth is hidden; it is happening, but no one can see it. Other stages are quite visible, even spectacular. Each stage has its purpose, each stage is necessary.

The way a child relates to God will be influenced by his age and developmental stage.

For example, very young children are quick to imitate what those around them are doing. So their behavior toward God will largely be shaped by simple imitation. If you bow your head during grace at dinner time, they will naturally follow suit. This doesn't make the action invalid; it's appropriate for their age.

By the same token, a two-year-old who suddenly refuses to bow his head at grace is not likely entering into significant rebellion against God, or refusal to honor him. He's probably just beginning to test the limits, assert his independence and the issue is incidental.

Similarly, very young children are inclined to accept as true what they are told. So their faith, from our perspective, can seem to come too easily. We might even be inclined not to take it seriously, as if it has no value. It's true that their faith is not tested to the degree that it will be. But it remains genuine faith.

As children grow older, they will naturally begin to question things which they had earlier simply accepted at face value. Their ability to think abstractly has probably matured to the point where they can even entertain questions in their minds. These questions don't necessarily represent a serious challenge to faith, they are a normal part of taking hold of what they believe.

With each new phase of personal growth, they will need new equipment to believe and obey. For several years, the opinions of peers will have relatively little impact on what children think. Their primary frame of reference will be derived from their parents. But by the age of nine or ten years, peer influence will become a much more important factor for them. And, of course, during adolescence the call of the peer group will become a very powerful force to contend with.

Helping them to find friends who share beliefs will be more important than it was before. And they will have a greater need to learn what it means to stand alone in their convictions for the sake of the truth, rather than to bend to the influence of peers. It will be important to discuss these things with them as the peer factor becomes a more powerful influence.

The growth of conscience is another important factor in a child's development. I can remember how surprised I was that our first two children seemed not to be "bothered" when they did something wrong. I think it would have been easy to view this as a defect in their relationship with God.

But the fact is, their conscience hadn't yet matured. They didn't have a strong interior voice that gave them a distaste for doing wrong. Their primary motivation was fear of getting caught. Their apologies for wrongdoing were not especially heartfelt. This didn't mean they were spiritually hard-hearted, just immature. They were living without the benefit of a well-formed conscience.

God created human beings to mature over a fairly long period of time, compared with other creatures. He is involved with us through every phase of development; he doesn't wait until we are humanly mature to begin to work with us. And his expectations of us and the activity of his Spirit in us differ according to where we are in the process of developing.

The parable of the mustard seed points to another important lesson in a child's relationship to God. There is a delay between planting and reaping. Sometimes the delay is relatively short, but sometimes it is seemingly interminable. Often the words or actions of parents or youth leaders— seeds of the kingdom planted in the hearts of young people—seem to go in one ear and out the other.

Rarely does a young person say to his father, "Thanks Dad. I think you've just given me a life-changing perspective." Rather, much of the growth is hidden beneath the surface. It may be many long years before certain lessons taught by a parent "break ground" in a young person's life and become visible to the light of day. The less we look for instant gratification, the more likely we will be to keep on sowing for a future harvest.

FIVE

Leading Young People to Jesus

IT WAS QUITE A SIGHT. Fifty young people, many with their fathers or mothers, talking and praying in small groups throughout the large room.

In each group, the young people took turns to individually express their decision to follow Jesus. They each renounced sin and the powers of darkness, asked Jesus to exercise his lordship over them, and gave themselves in love to him. There was an air of solemnity, but the mood was relaxed.

After each had confessed his or her faith to the rest of the group, it was time to pray over each one with the laying on of hands—in this case, an informal expression of blessing. Each young person then asked to be filled with the Spirit. Again, the atmosphere was not tense and anxious, nor was it emotionally charged. But God was moving gently among the young people and pouring out his Spirit. Some appeared to be visibly moved, others not. But when the time was completed, everyone felt that something very important and good had transpired.

Afterwards the parents especially were beaming. Many had begun the process wondering whether or not they were really competent to lead children into this personal commitment to Christ and prayer for empowerment. But after some simple instruction and a word or two of prompting, the parents were fully involved. All of them were praying with their children, laying hands on them and asking for the Spirit to descend. Before long, everyone realized what should have been obvious: on-going conversion is the work of the Holy Spirit. The leading and praying part is really quite easy.

The same experience of leading children to Jesus can happen in many different settings—one-on-one, in families, or in groups. In this chapter, we will consider how adults can lead young people in responding to the gospel in the context of presenting the material in Part Two of this book. You will have an opportunity to put this into practice in the dedication session described in chapter five of Part Two.

DON'T ASSUME SKEPTICISM

I've spent the last twenty years of my life in Ann Arbor, home to a major university, the University of Michigan. It was founded as the first secular state university in the country. The intellectual environment is quite comfortable with the idea that the pursuit of knowledge can be separated from the pursuit of God, and that humanity is the ultimate measure of all things. You might easily imagine that the social climate of Ann Arbor is riddled with skepticism concerning the kingdom of God.

So it is quite natural for me to expect anyone I speak to about matters of Christian faith to be skeptical. It's easy for me to anticipate objections and tailor my speech accordingly.

But it's important to realize that young people are not skeptics. They may have all kinds of questions to ask, but they don't normally approach the truth with their guard up.

Of course this is not to say that hardened young skeptics cannot be found in Christian homes. They can. But for the most part, simple belief in the basic facts of Christianity is not a major struggle for young people when they are presented with the truth. They are not nearly so inclined to doubt as adults are. Even when they choose to ignore the implications of the truth or struggle with conflicting pressures within and without, they are usually not nearly as skeptical as you might expect.

Because children have not erected as many intellectual barriers against the truth, you can begin with simple explanations of the truth, taking questions and concerns as they come. You may be surprised at how readily the truth is accepted.

Keep in mind that the questions coming from young people don't represent the same challenge to faith that questions coming from an adult might signal. Always treat their questions with respect. Take the time to give thoughtful consideration and offer your best answers. When you don't have a good answer, have the humility to say so: "That's a good question, I'll have to give that some more thought."

When speaking with teenagers and precocious younger minds, more attention to apologetics—dealing with the tough questions—is needed. There are several good resources available (for example, *Evidence That Demands a Verdict* by Josh McDowell).

CHILDREN HEAR AND UNDERSTAND
MORE THAN YOU THINK

If children are not as skeptical as you might think, they are also not as dumb as you might think. In fact, they are quite capable of grasping spiritual truth.

The problem is that young people are not in the habit of letting you know what they think about these kinds of issues. They are not inclined to nod their heads vigorously as you explain what it means to follow Jesus, then when you've made your point exclaim, "What an insight! Boy, that really opens it up for me!"

Remember that young people haven't developed a vocabulary for speaking about their spiritual experience and understanding. Often they are reluctant to talk about even very powerful encounters with God.

Tom is a good example of this reluctance. He's a young man who has had two very profound spiritual experiences. At the age of four years, an angel appeared to him. He shared this with his family. Then at the age of ten, he had an extremely vivid dream of Jesus coming to him. He saw what he thought was an angel walk into the room. Tom asked who the visitor was. The man showed him the wounds in his hands and side. Tom then peppered him with questions, "If you are Jesus, who did I have lunch with yesterday?" Each question was answered correctly. Jesus then took Tom through a door to the outside where he saw his house surrounded by an army of angels. With that, the visit ended.

The encounter was very striking, but Tom didn't tell anyone about it. He is a quiet young man and it was probably just too embarrassing to describe, even to his family—perhaps especially to his family. It didn't come out until several years later, when Tom's father was recounting an extraordinary angelic visitation that he had heard of. Even then, it was not an easy thing for Tom to talk about.

Tom's experience, as far as I know, is not unheard of—but it certainly is extraordinary. I'm not suggesting that your child or some young person you know is likely to see angels—but they *might!* When speaking with young people about the things of God, there is always a serious temptation to presume that too little is possible for them: "Oh, they'll never understand this, they could never experience that." Often that presumption is wrong.

Instead, we found it important to speak with a confident expectation that God will in fact work in them and through them. For example, when speaking about being filled with the Spirit, we would tend to say, "When you are filled with the Spirit," rather than "If you are filled with the Spirit." Of course, this needs to be held in balance with the fact that the young people do have the choice to ask or not.

Obviously, hyped-up, exaggerated expectations—especially those focused on subjective experience—are not helpful. Remember that for children raised in Christian homes, dramatic conversion experiences are not common. So avoid the kind of promises that are not likely to fit their experience, such as: "When you give yourself to Christ, he is going to revolutionize your life. You'll never be the same."

When presenting the truth to young people, be sure to stand on the authority of God's word. Make it clear that you are not giving your own thoughts and opinions, but sharing God's word. We've tried to select short, simple, and clear biblical texts which don't require lengthy explanation or interpretation to understand. God's word has a power that touches the heart of young people. It has the "ring of truth" to the heart that is open. So don't skim over the Scripture verses for fear that they will be "boring" to young people. If anything, highlight them: "This is what God says."

MAKE THE CHOICE CLEAR

My wife, Nancy, had a vivid dream the other night. In the dream Jesus came to her and said, "Tell (one of our daughters) that she has a choice." That was all that Nancy could remember from the dream, but it left quite an impression.

Young people need to know that they have a choice. In other words, being a Christian is not like being an American or a Canadian; it's not something you are simply born into. It involves a personal response to a personal invitation from Jesus to follow him and live as his disciple.

The focus of this book is not on raising children in the Christian faith—a process involving the whole of life—but on leading them to a personal commitment to Jesus and receiving an impartation of the promised Holy Spirit. When you are living together as a Christian family, the focus is, quite properly, "This is something we are doing together; we are a Christian family." So you don't ask each of the children every evening, "Do you choose to join us in giving thanks before dinner?" Nor do you say to a ten-year-old, "Would you like to come to church with us? It's your choice."

But children need to realize that there is more to being a Christian than living in a Christian family. As they grow older, their capacity to choose increases. This capacity is something they alone can exercise, under the influence of God's grace; and it is something they need to learn to exercise. For the very young child, this capacity is not well developed; he or she will likely follow along without much deep thought. That will do for a young child, but it won't do for a teenager.

The kind of response called for in the dedication session requires the young person to exercise his or her own capacity to choose, whatever that may be. The steps of drawing near to God covered in chapter ten in Part Two should be presented as an opportunity, an invitation, not something anyone can force them to do.

While stressing the reality of the young person's choice, it would be a big mistake to give the impression that these are simply matters of personal preference, like selecting a pair of shoes to buy. These are matters of eternal consequence. In the Book of Deuteronomy, the Lord said to the people of Israel, "I have set before you life and death. . . . Choose life!" (Deuteronomy 30:19).

FEELINGS

Young people, no less than adults, need help in understanding how to evaluate what occurs when they give their lives to Jesus and receive the gift of the Spirit. Did it really happen? How do I know I'm really forgiven? How do I know that I've received the Holy Spirit?

We've found it helpful to stress that the steps toward God are all in response to God's clear revelation in Scripture. In repenting, giving our lives to him, and so on, we are not acting on our own initiative, but on his. These are steps he is inviting us to take. Therefore we can count on him to respond according to his promises.

So ultimately we can only know that we are forgiven, or have received the Spirit, or anything else in the Christian life by faith in God and in his word. This is a more certain guide to evaluating what occurs than our subjective experience or feelings.

While it is important to allow for the valid place of feelings and other subjective phenomenon, these should not become the basis for measuring God's action. Certain feelings and experiences are common, but they are not the goal in themselves. And it is also possible for people to experience little in the way of feelings, yet have a genuine work of the Spirit within them.

THE SPIRITUAL BATTLE

When I was ready to give my life to the Lord as a nineteen-year-old, I called a Christian friend late at night to ask him what I should do. While he was speaking to me on the phone, a cross and a picture of Christ hanging on his wall fell off with no apparent explanation. Fortunately I had no idea this was happening, but it was pretty spooky for him. Whenever anyone seeks to draw near to God, some kind of spiritual resistance from the powers of darkness can be anticipated.

When leading young people to Jesus, it is important to take a special concern to pray for spiritual protection for all those concerned. It is good for the participants to know that God has an enemy in the spiritual realm who seeks to destroy his work, who sows confusion and doubt. Especially during the time immediately preceding and following the dedication session, this can be anticipated.

Deal with this factor straightforwardly and in faith: "Resist the devil and he will flee from you. Come near to God and he will come near to you" (James 4:7-8). If you feel that specific prayers of deliverance (or binding of the work of evil spirits) are called for, by all means proceed with confidence in the power of Jesus' name.

TELL YOUR STORY

If you help your son or daughter or another young person to respond to the offer of life in the Spirit, you will be presented with a wonderful opportunity to share from your own experience. What were the circumstances that led to your becoming a Christian or taking a step closer to God or responding to his call? When you were a young person, how were you aware of God's presence? How has Jesus worked in the lives of family members or friends?

When young people are considering these issues for themselves, they are likely to be more interested in the experiences of others. Parents are often surprised to find that their children have never heard about some significant personal experiences with God. So go ahead and tell them.

PART TWO

Receiving the Promise:

For Young People Ready to Get on with the Greatest Adventure of Their Lives

"Seek and you will find; knock and the door will be opened to you." **Luke 11:9**

SIX

God's Love

HAS THE THOUGHT EVER CROSSED YOUR MIND that God must not be interested in showing himself to you? I call that thought the "big lie."

Think about the television shows you watch or the movies you've seen. How many were about someone your age getting to know God? That's the big lie at work.

Or think about a typical day at many schools. How often is God mentioned (not counting the curses out on the playground)? Not very often. That's the big lie at work again.

GOD'S INTEREST IN YOUNG PEOPLE

But in spite of the big lie, God is interested in showing himself to young people—and he does.

My friend had a seven-year-old brother, named Benjamin. This young boy became very sick. He lived in India and didn't have a chance to see a doctor. One night Benjamin had a very high fever and his breathing became very light, and he wasn't moving much at all. He was asleep when he should have been awake, and no one could rouse him.

Suddenly, he woke up and his eyes became bright and clear. He looked at his mother, who was nearby, then looked up toward the ceiling, lifting up his arms—like a young child would lift up his arms to be picked up by his dad. In a strong voice, the young boy cried out "Jesus!" and then he died.

This young boy saw Jesus just before he died. Benjamin was the youngest of many children, and he was still at that age when kids are pretty attached to their mothers. My friend was amazed that even though his mother was nearby, Benjamin did not cry out "Mommy!" when he died, but "Jesus!"

My son Jesse has a friend named Chris. Chris's mom had a disease of the bladder. The doctors didn't have any cure. She asked a friend to come over one day to pray with her. Chris joined with the friend to pray for his mom. At one point, the friend said to Chris, "I think the Lord wants you to place your hand on your mom's stomach and pray for her bladder to get better right now." Chris gave him a look that said, "Who, me?" (The big lie was at work again.)

"Yes, you."

Chris placed his hand on his mom's stomach, and the words that came out of his mouth surprised Chris and everyone else.

"Bladder, I'm telling you in the name of Jesus—be healed."

Immediately, his mother felt a sensation of warmth in her bladder and the pain and other symptoms went away. She was cured.

Now those are two pretty dramatic examples. But the point is a simple one. God is interested in showing himself to you now. He doesn't have to wait until you're finished with high school, or about to get married, or having children of your own.

A Young Prophet. In the time of the Bible there was a boy named Samuel, who lived in the Temple area. One night he heard a voice calling in the dark: "Samuel!" He thought it was Eli, in the other room next to his. But Eli was asleep. Samuel woke him up and said, "Why did you call me?" Eli said, "You're dreaming! I didn't call you. I was asleep until you woke me up. Go back to bed!"

You may know the story. This happened two more times. Each time, Samuel went back to bed, heard the voice calling him and woke up Eli. Eventually Samuel realized that the voice was the voice of God. But it was hard to believe at first. The big lie must have been around then too.

A Young Warrior. David was the youngest of several brothers. He was too young to join the army of Israel, which was at war with the Philistines. He went to visit his brothers near the battlefield, and what he discovered there made him pretty angry. Goliath, a huge Philistine warrior, was mocking the God of Israel, taunting the soldiers of Israel to fight him one on one. But the whole army was frightened by Goliath.

David—a young teenager—took up the challenge. He believed that God would work through him to defeat Goliath. David's older brothers didn't believe that God could use someone so young (the big lie again). Of course Goliath, at the sight of young David mocked all the more.

"You send this boy to fight with me? Is this the best mighty Israel can come up with?"

But David, with no armor and only a few stones and a sling for a weapon, stood up to Goliath and defeated him. A great victory for Israel's army, all because of the faith of a boy.

A Teenage Girl. Or remember Mary, the mother of Jesus. How old do you think she was when the angel came to her and asked her to assent to God's plan to send Jesus into the world through her? Thirty-five? Twenty-four? Nineteen? Mary may have been as young as thirteen at the time.

Jesus and Young People. Even the first followers of Jesus listened to the big lie. Once a group of young children crowded around Jesus. The disciples saw the commotion and began to yell at the kids and the people who brought them: "Don't bother the master with those kids!" But Jesus became angry with the disciples and told them to back off, to let the children come near him. Then he put his hands on each child and blessed and spoke with them all.

The idea that God is not interested in showing himself to young people is nothing but a lie. You have an opportunity, if you wish, to take some steps closer to God (more about that in a later chapter). But more importantly, God is ready to take some steps closer to you.

GOD'S INTEREST IN YOU

To begin with, let's consider some important things about God and you.

Let's begin with you. Where did you come from? Hasn't that question sneaked up on you a few times already? You're lying in your bed, not feeling very sleepy and the thought pops into your mind, "Where did I come from anyway? Who made me? And why?"

Where *did* you come from? Well, you could say that you came from your mother and father. And that would be true. Your mother and father came together and you were born. But it's not the whole truth, is it? Your mother and father may have decided to have a baby, but who decided that that baby should be you... a boy or a girl, with a certain color hair and eyes, a certain kind of person different than anyone else ever made? Your mother and father didn't sit down and put you together like a jigsaw puzzle or fashion you out of a piece of clay.

Do you think you "just happened," or do you think someone made you, created you? Think about a watch or a televison set. Those are pretty interesting things. Did they just happen, or did someone make them? The answer is obvious.

You are at least as interesting as a wristwatch or a television set. Much more impressive, in fact, and valuable. Whoever made you must be the most powerful being in the whole universe. In fact that's exactly who made you. God did. No other answer makes very much sense, does it?

Next question: if God made you, why did he make you?

The answer is simple. God made you because he wanted you. Because he cares about you. Because he loves you.

God so loved the world that he gave his one and only Son, that whoever believes in him shall not perish but have eternal life. John 3:16

Maybe there have been times when you thought you were so ugly, or dumb, or awful that no one, especially not God, could love you—not if they really knew you. Or maybe you thought you were just too boring for God to be interested in you.

Well, God knows you better than anyone else knows you. Better than you know yourself. He knows you because he made you. And he made you because he loves you.

FRIENDS WITH GOD

God loves you. That's pretty good news, but it gets even better. Not only does he love you, but he wants to have a friendship with you.

> Greater love has no one than this, that one lay down his life for his friends. You are my friends if you do what I command. I no longer call you servants, because a servant does not know his master's business. Instead, I have called you friends. John 15:13-15

Jesus wants to call you his friend. In other words, he wants to know you personally, to have a personal relationship with you.

What is a personal relationship? It means knowing someone well, and being known by that person. You don't have a personal relationship with the Channel 7 weatherman. You probably don't have a personal relationship with the President of the United States. You have a personal relationship with people whom you know and who know you, like your parents, your sister or brother, your aunt and uncle, your next-door neighbor, your friends, your teacher at school, your grandfather or grandmother.

Think of it. God wants to have a personal relationship with you. He already knows you, and he wants you to know him. He wants a friendship with you.

LIFE TO THE FULL

The good news just got better, but it is better yet. God loves you and he wants a friendship with you, but he also wants to give you a better life.

Jesus said, "I have come that [you] may have life, and have it to the full" (John 10:10).

Every human being has life, but Jesus wants to give us life "to the full." He wants to give us an overflowing life. He wants to give us a better life, a higher life than we have on our own.

We all know that there are different kinds of life—some are better, higher, more full (in a sense, more alive) than others. For example a blade of grass can be alive. But it is one thing to be alive like a blade of grass and another to be alive like a small creature—say, a worm. A worm is a higher, better form of life than a blade of grass. There's more to a worm, it does more things than a blade of grass can do. It can move, and eat, and feel the earth.

And of course, a dog is a better form of life than a worm. A dog can bark and be excited, and play, and hunt, and swim, and chase cats. A human being is the highest form of life among the creatures God has made.

But even human beings can have more life or less life. Some years ago, my father got very sick and went into a coma. A person in a coma is deeply asleep and cannot wake up. When my father was in a coma, the doctor would poke him with a sharp needle, but he wouldn't even move, because he couldn't feel the pain. He was alive, but not very alive.

Jesus came to give us a better life, life to the full. He wants to give us a life that won't wear out after seventy-five years, a life that will not die, but go on forever. Eventually, he wants to give us a brand new body that will make our present bodies seem like an old, rusty car with blue smoke coming out of the tailpipe. In the meantime, he wants to give us a new and better life within, so that we can be more and more like him.

By the way, my father got completely better, even though

the doctors said he would be damaged for life if he ever did wake up. When he woke up, he gave his life to Jesus (he wasn't a Christian when he got sick), because he knew the Lord had spared him. But that's another story.

A SERIOUS DECISION

So God loves us and he wants to have a friendship with us. He wants to give us more life, a better life, an overflowing life that will never end. But there is something else we should know about God. The God who loves us is also an awesome, righteous God. He has all power in the universe. He is a mighty King who expects human beings to accept him and obey him. Knowing and loving God the Father and his Son, the Lord Jesus Christ is the best thing that could happen to anyone in the world. But it is not a game. In fact, it is a matter of life and death.

> For God so loved the world that he gave his one and only Son that whoever believes in him shall not perish but have eternal life . . . Whoever believes in him is not condemned, but whoever does not believe stands condemned already because he has not believed in the name of God's one and only Son. John 3:16, 18

Jesus spoke of two different paths—one that leads to life, eternal life, heaven; and another that leads to death, eternal death, hell. The thing that makes heaven heaven is the fact that God, the source of all life, is there. The thing that makes hell hell is the fact that God is not there. His absence leaves only death, pain, and suffering.

We are either heading in one direction or the other—toward God, toward heaven, or away from God, toward hell. Jesus is the only one who can show us the way to the Father, to life, to heaven. He's been there, that's where he came from, and he's the only one who knows the way. So you can see that this is not a big game. We don't decide to follow Jesus like we might decide to cheer for a particular baseball team—as if it's all just for fun and not serious business. This is serious business, the most serious business of all. It's a matter of life and death.

STEPS TOWARD LIFE

In a few weeks, you will have an opportunity to take another step toward life. You will be able to give your life to Jesus, and for many that will mean simply saying, "Yes" again to Jesus.

You will also have the opportunity to be prayed with to be filled with the Holy Spirit, to receive more of the life that Jesus came to give us.

In the meantime, I would like to ask you to do two things. These are quite simple, but will help you to draw closer to God during this time.

First of all, remember what we have already talked about. Ignore that big lie that says God is not interested in people until they are adults. Remember the truth instead: God loves you and wants a friendship with you. He wants to give you more life than you have now, better life, overflowing life. And all this life comes from Jesus.

Second, each day between now and the time you finish this book, give God five minutes of your time. In section three of this book, you will find short meditations for each day of the week. They are labelled one through five for this chapter. Find a quiet place, away from noisy brothers or sisters, definitely away from the television set, or anything else that might distract you. If your day is too busy, stay up a little later and take your time with God just before you fall asleep. Read the meditation for the day and pray the prayer that is suggested at the end of each one.

(NOTE: After this chapter, you may want to turn to page 163 and read "Dan's Story," a short testimony by a teenager who came to know how much God loved him.)

STUDENTS ARE TO
READ DAN'S STORY
AT HOME. SUNDAY.
MONDAY "THE GIFT"
TUESDAY "FRIENDS"
WEDNESDAY "POWER TO LIVE"
THURSDAY "ANYBODY HOME?"
FRIDAY "ASK"

SEVEN

What's Wrong?

A S YOU'VE GOTTEN OLDER, you've begun to notice something you would rather not discover. You can try to ignore it or hide from it, but it's still there. Something is wrong with the world, seriously wrong.

THE BAD NEWS EXPLOSION

Just the other day I watched the local late-night news. First, I heard about a teenager who had been shot by another teenager that day. Then there was a report about a local hospital that cared for babies born to women who were on drugs. The babies were born addicted to drugs through the mothers.

The next story was about a group of people protesting the abortion of twenty-six million unborn babies. After the commercial (no bad news there), the newswoman told about the troubles in the city schools. Over half the students were dropping out of school before graduation. Everyone was quite concerned, but no one knew how to solve the problem. I'd heard enough news for the night!

This was just the news for one night, in one city. All over

the country that night—in fact, all over the world, the same kinds of things were happening. And it's not new. This didn't just start last year. Things are seriously wrong all over the world and they have been wrong for a long time.

About a hundred years ago many people thought that human life was getting better and better. It was just a matter of time, until sickness would be eliminated and wars would cease. Or so they thought.

Then World War I came along—killing millions of soldiers and ordinary citizens. Twenty years later, World War II broke out, and it was worse. By the end of that war, human beings learned how to make nuclear bombs so that now we have the power to blow up all the cities on the earth. Twenty years later Americans were sending some men into outer space, while black Americans were being brutalized for trying to vote in the South.

No wonder people turn off the television when the news comes on! But turning off the televison doesn't solve the problem. Something's wrong with the whole world, and it comes around to our home, our family, our relatives, our friends, ourselves.

Just the other day, I had one of those bad news days myself: I heard about a friend who was getting a divorce, my daughter was playing in the gym and broke something in her knee, and then we had a big rainstorm and my basement flooded. I didn't need to watch the news that night to know that something is seriously wrong with the world!

You know what I'm talking about. Maybe you had a favorite grandmother who died. Or perhaps someone in your family has been very sick. Or any number of other things have made you angry or sad or disappointed, so you understand my point.

The question we all ask is, why? Why do all these bad

things happen? Why is something wrong with the world? How did we get into this mess?

Different people give different answers to this question. Some people say something's wrong because we don't have enough money, or because people need more or better education. But these answers are not complete.

GOD'S POINT OF VIEW

What does God have to say about how we got into this mess?

First of all God says that when he first created the world, there was nothing wrong with it. It was beautiful. Everything worked. Nothing was broken. Nothing got old or died.

At first, man and woman were good. They had no problems, no troubles, no sickness, no fighting. It was heaven on earth. But then man and woman decided they didn't really need God anymore. They could do things their own way and ignore what God said.

It didn't work. Worse than that, it ruined everything. On the side of a milk carton it says, "Keep in the refrigerator." What happens if you ignore that advice and leave the milk on the counter overnight? It goes sour. It begins to smell bad. You can't use it anymore.

That's what happened to the world because of humanity's disobedience to God. Things went sour. From that point on, evil and sickness, war and suffering and trouble began to take over.

We're all part of the mess and it is a big mess, isn't it? A big problem needs a big solution. All of the solutions that we can think up on our own are too small. They may help a little, but with a problem this big, a little is not enough. You can't cure cancer with a couple of aspirins or fix a broken arm by putting on a Band-Aid.

In the comic books or on the cartoons, when people are in a big mess, Superman, Spiderman, Batman, Superwoman, or Prince Valiant comes to save them. But we're talking about real life, not a game or a cartoon. Pretending won't work; we need a real solution. We need God to give us the answer, to save us from this mess.

GOD'S SOLUTION

After all this bad news, don't you think it's time for some good news? The good news is this: God has given us the Big Solution that we need to the Big Problem. It's the good news (or the gospel) of Jesus Christ. This good news can be summed up in four spiritual laws.

1. God Loves You and Has a Wonderful Plan for Your Life. "I know the plans I have for you," declares the Lord, "plans to prosper you and not to harm you" (Jeremiah 29:11).

When God created you he had something special in mind. He has a plan for your life, a special purpose. He didn't create you like one of those wind-up toys that you just crank up and let go. There's a reason he created you. Now that he's made you, he wants to lead you and guide you into his plan for your life.

Some things about God's plan for your life are already known because they are the same for everyone: things like God created you to love him, to love other people.

Some other things God wants to show you over time. You will discover what his plan is. For example he has given or will give you certain gifts that you can use to serve him and other people. Maybe his plan for you is to be a teacher, or to be a missionary, a doctor, or a mother. Perhaps he will use you to bring healing to other people, or you will help people who need a home, or food to eat. Perhaps you will bring God's message to others.

Of course, this doesn't mean that you won't have any serious troubles in your life. Jesus said, "In this world, you will have trouble" (John 16:33). But he promises to be with you in trouble and even to use those troubles to work out his plan for good.

Now if God loves people and has a wonderful plan for their lives, how is it that we don't know what that plan is? Why do so many people seem to miss out on that plan? That brings us to the Second Spiritual Law.

2. We Have Been Separated from God and His Plan through Sin. "For all have sinned and fall short of the glory of God" (Romans 3:23).

"Return . . . to the Lord your God. Your sins have been your downfall!" (Hosea 14:1).

Imagine a group of Indians or early settlers approaching the Grand Canyon for the first time. They had never heard of it, never seen any postcards, didn't know it was there. The Canyon plunged down so far that it made them all dizzy. It stretched as far as the eye could see to the left and to the right. And it was so far across to the other side!

First someone in the group threw a stone into the Canyon. But no one even saw or heard it hit bottom. Then an archer shot an arrow to the other side. But the arrow didn't come close, and fell down to the canyon floor. No one even thought of jumping across or throwing a rope to the other side. Everyone just stood there at the edge of the canyon, with their mouths wide open. Then they sat down and did the only thing they could do—scratched their heads.

The separation between God and human beings caused by sin makes the Grand Canyon look like a crack in the pavement. The gap is so great we cannot hope to cross it by ourselves. There is nothing we can do on our own about it.

Oh, we can try, but it won't work.

Trying hard to be good doesn't close the gap.

Pretending the gap isn't really there doesn't make it go away.

Throwing a fit, jumping up and down screaming, "It's not fair!" doesn't work.

Neither does wishing on a star.

So why not just give up? Why not sit down and say, "Forget about God! What's the use?"

This brings us to the Third Spiritual Law.

3. The Father Has Provided Jesus to Bridge the Gap Between Us and Himself. Jesus said, "I am the way and the truth and the life. No one comes to the Father except through me" (John 14:6).

Let's go back to those Indians sitting on one side of the Grand Canyon for the first time, scratching their heads. Now imagine some activity far across on the other side. They all stand up to look. A bridge begins to take shape on the other side. This bridge is not the work of human hands. There are no cranes, or workmen, or bulldozers, or supervisors running around. Just a bridge rising out of the ground extending across the canyon toward them!

It would take a miracle like that, an act of God, to bring

those Indians across to the other side. And it took a miracle, an act of God, to bridge the gap between God and human beings that was caused by human sin.

The miracle is Jesus, sent by the Father to the other side, into the world. Jesus is the bridge. He brings God to us and us to God. He brings heaven to earth, and makes a way for us to go to heaven.

When Jesus came into the world, the people who saw him were drawn to him. Wherever he went, the crowds came too. Often there were so many people around him that he had to get onto a boat and speak to the people from the boat out on the water.

He didn't run any commercials on television. He didn't place any advertisements in the newspapers to draw such a crowd. They just came to him, wherever he was.

Why did they come to him? Why have people been coming to Jesus by the thousands and millions all over the world for the past two thousand years—confessing their sins to him, giving their lives to him? Not just because he works miracles and heals people—though that will usually draw a crowd. Not just to hear his teaching—though that will draw a crowd too.

Something else draws people to Jesus. Whether they know it or not, human beings are hungry for God. Even if we are fearful of God, or if we have doubts that he exists, still we have a strong desire for God himself. We want to know him, we want to feel his presence, we want to be with him.

We are like the fish who always swim back, year after year, to the place they were hatched. Or the geese who fly back, year after year, thousands of miles to the same patch of land. We are like the orphan who goes out in search of his lost family. When we are away from home, sooner or later we want to go back. And our home is with God, more than any place else, because we were created by God, we come from him.

When Jesus showed up two thousand years ago, people were drawn to him because deep inside they knew that Jesus could bring them back to God, back to the Father. Jesus could bring them to heaven. He could bring them home.

And they were right. Jesus is the way across that huge gap between us and God. We couldn't do anything to close that gap, so God did it for us, by sending his Son, Jesus.

How does Jesus bring us back to the Father, how does he bridge the gap? He does it in three ways.

1. Jesus bridges the gap by showing us who God is and what he is like. When you are separated from someone for a long, long time, you begin to forget what that person looks like. Because the gap between God and human beings is so wide, we've gotten all sorts of funny ideas about what God is like:

- Some of us think that God is like Santa Claus—a jolly old man with red cheeks, who shows up once a year to give us presents.

- Some of us think that God is like an overly strict teacher who always seems mad at her class. Nothing anyone can do ever seems to satisfy her.

- Some of us think that God changes from day to day— like the weather. One day he loves us, the next day he couldn't care less. One day he's strong and powerful, the next day he's weak.

- Some of us think that God is nothing more than the Keeper of the Rules. The only thing he does is lay down the rules to keep track of the times we break them.

All those ideas about what God is like don't hit the nail on the head. They don't give a clear and accurate picture of who God is. Only Jesus gives us that clear picture: "He is the image of the invisible God" (Colossians 1:15).

If we want to know what God is like, there is only one true picture—look to see what Jesus is like.

2. Jesus bridges the gap between God and human beings by taking on himself the punishment for our sins. God is merciful and loving, but he is also just. That means that sin must be punished. There is a penalty for sin and the penalty must be paid. Unfortunately for us, the penalty for sin is death. As soon as man began to sin, he began to die.

Jesus came to pay the penalty for us. When Jesus died on the cross, he died for us. He died in our place. We deserved to be crucified, as he was. We deserved to be separated from God, but Jesus took our place.

3. Jesus bridges the gap between God and human beings by giving us a new power to live the way God wants us to live. It's not enough simply to know how God wants us to live. We also need the power to do it. Jesus gives us that power. We'll talk more about this in the next chapter.

If Jesus is the way back to God, if he is the bridge across the gap, how do we make the journey? How do we cross over? That brings us to the Fourth Spiritual Law.

4. We Must Accept Jesus as Our Lord and Savior. Once we know that God loves us enough to give his Son Jesus as the bridge over the gap that separates us from God, we have to do something about it. Just sitting on your bicycle doesn't get you to your friend's house. You have to ride the bike. Standing on one side of a bridge doesn't get you across. You have to walk across (or drive).

How do we cross the bridge? How does Jesus become the way *for us*? By accepting Jesus as our Lord and Savior.

What does it mean to accept Jesus as your Lord? It means agreeing that he is in charge and being willing to do what he says. When you join an organized baseball team (or any other team), you have to agree to do whatever the coach tells you to do—at least when it comes to playing baseball on his team. If he tells you to play shortstop, you don't go out into right field. If he tells you to take the fourth position in the batting order, you can't lead off, just because you feel like batting first.

To accept Jesus as your Lord means agreeing to do whatever he tells you to do.

What does it mean to accept Jesus as your Savior?

It simply means accepting his gifts with gratitude. You probably haven't thought much about not accepting a gift. When has the thought ever occurred to you to say, "No. I don't think I will accept any of my Christmas gifts this year."

But there are times when people have a difficult time accepting a gift. Adults tend to do this more than children, which is probably why Jesus told adults that to enter his kingdom they had to become like children. Have you ever seen two businessmen going out to lunch together? At the end of the meal, the waitress brings the check. One man picks up the check and says, "I'll pay for lunch." The other man grabs for the check and says, "No! Don't do that. I'll pay!"

Once a friend of mine offered to give me some money. I needed the money. I even wanted the money, once he made the offer. But I stood there saying, "Oh no, I couldn't let you do that." We stood there and argued for a few minutes. "Take it!" "No, I can't!" "Yes you can, just take it!" I can't remember whether or not I received the gift.

Another time I was working for a magazine, helping to write the articles. My boss came to my desk and said, "You did a great job on this last issue. You are an excellent writer." What did I say, in response? "It was OK, but it wasn't really that good—at least I didn't think so." I went on like this until the secretary for the magazine chimed in, "Ken, *receive* the compliment."

To accept Jesus as our Savior means accepting the gift of salvation. It means accepting the gift of forgiveness of our sins. It means accepting the fact that he paid the penalty for our sins. It means saying, "Thanks, I needed that. And I gladly receive it from you as a gift."

Accepting a gift isn't a difficult thing to do. It just means opening your hand and saying, "Yes" and then, "Thank you." It's not difficult, but it is necessary. If you don't accept a gift, you won't get it.

Jesus said, "I stand at the door and knock. If anyone hears my voice and opens the door, I will come in and eat with him, and he with me" (Revelation 3:20).

He gives the gift, he knocks on the door. But we need to accept the gift, to open the door and let him in.

In a later chapter, you will have a special opportunity to respond to this Fourth Spiritual Law about accepting Jesus as Lord and Savior. In the meantime, get acquainted with the Four Spiritual Laws. The Meditations section for daily prayer will focus on the Four Spiritual Laws, to help you understand them better and review what they are. Don't forget to give God five minutes of your time each day during the next week.

(NOTE: After this chapter, you may want to turn to page 167 and read "Robin's Story," a testimony by a thirteen-year-old boy who received a special gift from God.)

EIGHT

Knowing God

I N THE MOVIE, *Oh God!*, comedian George Burns plays God. He shows up looking like George Burns, smoking a cigar. He talks to people, does something spectacular, then disappears for a while.

George Burns is a good comedian, but a lousy God. He just doesn't have what it takes to run a universe. And the cigar doesn't make it either.

At the same time, a movie like that gets you thinking. Wouldn't it be great if God just "showed up" like George Burns does in the movie?

Wouldn't you like to see God? Yes, I mean actually see him, as you can see this page or the floor under your feet.

Wouldn't you like to shake hands with God?

Of course, you have never seen God, in the way you can see another human being. And you've never shaken hands with God either. It's probably just as well. Because if you really did see God in all his power and glory, you might not survive. You can't even look at the sun on a bright day without hurting your eyes. What do you think it would be like to look at God, who is much more powerful than the sun?

George Burns, playing God in a movie, is one thing. God himself—in all his glory—is quite another.

WHAT IS GOD LIKE?

Jesus said, "God is spirit" (John 4:24).

God is a different kind of being than we are. We are human beings, but God is spirit. At this point in time, we cannot see God, because he is spirit. "No one has ever seen God . . ." said the apostle John, and he was right. God is invisible.

When we speak of knowing God, or having a relationship with God, we can get frustrated if we think that relating to him is just like relating to any person. After all, it's *different* relating to someone you cannot see. You don't just walk up to God and tap him on the shoulder as you might do with your father to gain his attention. If you wonder whether your brother is in the house, you just look around until you see him. There he is, messing with your stuff again. When you see him, you know he's there. But it's different with God who is invisible.

So what does this mean, to say that God is spirit, that he is invisible? Does it mean he doesn't exist, just because we cannot see him? Of course not! There are many things in this world that exist even though we cannot see them. Take the wind for example.

I once woke up in the morning to the sound of several great, loud crashes. I looked out of the window and the sky was green. I ran downstairs and saw some huge trees fallen over across the street. It was as if some giant hand had taken hold of the trees by the trunk, pulled them out of the ground with a clump full of roots and set them down. Big trees, not little trees.

What caused all the commotion? The wind was blowing. About seventy-five miles per hour. Now, strictly speaking, I couldn't see the wind. But I sure knew it was there.

Because God is invisible he takes special care to reveal himself to us.

Just think if *you* were invisible. Of course, there are probably times when you wished you were invisible, like when you are getting caught in the act of doing something wrong, or when the teacher calls on you to do a math problem up at the board in front of the class. The math problem you forgot to study last night.

But imagine that you were invisible and you wanted people to know that you existed. In fact, you wanted people to know you and love you. What would you do? You would take steps to reveal yourself.

That's the way it is with God. He understands that mere human beings like you and me cannot hope to find him and know him and relate to him unless he reveals himself to us.

What steps has the invisible God taken to show himself to people like you and me, who are not particularly good at seeing what cannot be seen?

Step 1: God Reveals Himself in Creation. "Since the creation of the world God's invisible qualities—his eternal power and divine nature—have been clearly seen, being understood from what has been made" (Romans 1:20).

First of all, God created the universe and the world we live in to make constant suggestions to us about what he must be like.

The world around us is forever giving us big signals about God. Get away from the city lights some night when the sky is clear and look at the stars. Some of those little needle points of light are stars much bigger than our sun. Some of those stars have already burned themselves out. But you can still see them because it takes the light so long to reach us here on earth. Some of those stars are just the light leftover from a star that is now gone!

It doesn't take a genius to realize that whoever created all this must be extremely powerful, bigger than anyone can imagine.

Stop sometime to look at a flower garden in full bloom: roses, daisies, carnations, irises—all in different colors. Each one a work of art. Whoever created this world must be a great artist—not someone dull and boring, but someone very creative. Everyday, the creation bombards us with one sign after another about what God must be like. You don't even have to be looking for these things, they are staring you in the face everyday.

Step 2: God Reveals Himself in His Son. "No one has ever seen God, but God the only Son, who is at the Father's side, has made him known" (John 1:18).

The invisible God has taken a step to reveal himself to us by becoming a man in the person of Jesus Christ.

During the time when Jesus Christ lived in the land of Israel, men and women and children could see, touch, and hear God in human form.

A man who knew Jesus wrote this about him:

That which was from the beginning, which we have heard, which we have seen with our eyes, which we have looked at and our hands have touched—this we proclaim concerning the Word of Life. 1 John 1:1

This was a tremendous step forward in God's efforts to show himself to human beings. For the first time, people could see what God himself was like—-not just good hints about what he must be like, but God himself in the form of a person. Jesus revealed God not just by what he said, but by who he was: God in person.

That was all well and good for the people fortunate enough to live in Israel during the time of Christ's life on earth. But what about the rest of us, who were born years later, far away from the place Jesus lived?

Step 3: God Reveals Himself in His Word. God has revealed himself in his word, the Bible. The men and women who saw, heard, and touched Jesus left us some eyewitness accounts in the Bible, so that we could all come to know about Jesus, and through Jesus learn about God.

Someone has said that the Bible is a collection of God's love letters to his people. Others have said that the Bible is like a roadmap that shows us the way to heaven, or that the Bible is like one of those manufacturers' instruction manuals you get when you purchase a new television or washing machine. The Bible is God's way of telling us how we are to live and how we can know him.

Step 4: God Reveals Himself to Us in His Spirit. God reveals himself to us by giving us the Holy Spirit.

A lot of people think that the Christian faith is mainly about things that happened in the past: the stories in the Bible and the events of Jesus' life. Or it is easy to think of the Christian faith as mainly concerned about the future— meeting God in heaven when we die (someday!) or seeing Jesus return from heaven to earth at the end of the world (someday!)

Maybe you've had a conversation like this: "Hey Dad, let's go to Disneyworld!" "Sounds great. Maybe we will someday."

"Someday! When is Someday?"

While God's action in the past is very important, as well as his plan for the future, I will guess that the most important question in your mind right now is, "What about today? How can I know God today?"

It's good to know that God sent his Son, Jesus Christ, two thousand years ago, but I wasn't alive two thousand years ago. What about today? How does he communicate with me today? How does what he did through Jesus make a difference for me now?

God makes contact with you today through the gift of his Spirit to you.

The gift of the Holy Spirit to human beings is a very important part of God's plan for us. From the very beginning of time, God has wanted to make himself known to human beings through giving them his Spirit.

THE SPIRIT IN HISTORY

So that you can understand what God is up to today, let's take a brief detour and see how God has given his Spirit to human beings throughout history.

When the first humans were created, named Adam and Eve in the Book of Genesis (Adam means "Man" or "Mankind," Eve means "Woman"), how did God "get them started"? How did he make them alive?

The Lord God formed man . . . and breathed into his nostrils the breath of life, and man became a living being. **Genesis 2:7**

So man wasn't "wound up" like an alarm clock or a toy soldier. He wasn't "jump-started" like a car with a dead battery. He wasn't injected with a special medicine by hypodermic needle. No, it was a very personal thing. The Lord God came close to the man and breathed into him. That breath from God himself was his Spirit, and it made the man alive for the first time.

After death came into the world through man's sin, God gave his Spirit to certain individuals on rare occasions. For example, he gave his Spirit to men and women called "Prophets" who were then able to speak out a special message directly from God. He gave his Spirit to a man like King David, so that David could defeat the enemies of God's people and lead them.

God gave his Spirit in a special way to Moses, who received God's law for the people of Israel. One day, Moses realized he needed help to lead the people of Israel, he needed some assistants. So he called together seventy leading men and prayed that God would give them the same Spirit he had received. As soon as Moses prayed in that way, the Spirit came on the seventy men and they began to do something very unusual: they all began to prophesy—to speak aloud a message given directly from God.

Two of the seventy men didn't show up for the meeting where Moses prayed for the Spirit to come upon them. They were at home, minding their own business. But when Moses prayed, the Spirit came on them as well and they too began to prophesy. We don't know what they were doing at the time—mowing the lawn, having dinner with the family—but whatever it was, the Spirit came on them and they prophesied.

Someone objected to this, thinking it was a terrible thing that the Spirit should fall on these two men who were not even at the meeting. Who did they think they were anyway, receiving the Spirit of God and prophesying like that? This was reserved for special men like Moses, people thought. So they complained to Moses about this.

What did Moses do? Punish the men who prophesied for creating a disturbance? No, he said to those who complained, "Oh, I wish the Lord would put his Spirit on all of his people, and that they would all prophesy!"

See, Moses knew that the gift of the Holy Spirit would not always be restricted to a few special people. God had something big up his sleeve. He wanted to pour out his Spirit on anyone willing to receive the Spirit.

After hundreds of years when God only gave his Spirit to a few select people, Jesus arrived on the scene and things began to change dramatically.

JESUS' PROMISE OF THE SPIRIT

John the Baptist said of Jesus, "He will baptize you with the Holy Spirit." The word "baptize" means to dip something so that it is covered over completely, like a soft-serve ice cream cone dipped into a vat of chocolate so that it is covered completely with chocolate. Now that's a distracting thought!

As the time approached for Jesus to be crucified and raised from the dead, he spoke frequently about the Holy Spirit.

Now I am going to him who sent me. . . . But I tell you the truth: It is for your good that I am going away. Unless I go away, the Counselor will not come to you; but if I go, I will send him to you. John 16:5, 7

The "Counselor" is another name for the Holy Spirit. Jesus promised to send the Holy Spirit after he was raised from the dead and brought into heaven.

After Jesus was killed, then raised from the dead, he appeared alive to his disciples. Again he told them that the Holy Spirit would soon be sent to them.

Do not leave Jerusalem, but wait for the gift my Father promised, which you have heard me speak about. . . . in a few days, you will be baptized with the Holy Spirit. . . . You will receive power when the Holy Spirit comes on you. Acts 1:4-5, 8

THE SPIRIT'S ARRIVAL

You know what it is like to wait for a gift that you know is coming soon, like waiting for Christmas to come. It's exciting. It's something you look forward to. That's what it must have been like for the disciples. Except that they didn't know exactly what this gift of the Holy Spirit would be like. What happens when you receive a gift like this?

They found out a few days later on a holiday called "Pentecost." Here is what happened:

They were all together in one place. Suddenly a sound like the blowing of a violent wind came from heaven and filled the whole house where they were sitting. They saw what seemed to be tongues of fire that separated and came to rest on each of them. All of them were filled with the Holy Spirit and began to speak in other tongues [other languages] as the Spirit enabled them. Acts 2:1-4

The Book of Acts tells what happened when these men and women and children were filled with the Holy Spirit. Things changed for them. They had a new power at work in them.

What are some of those new things that happened? We will save that for our next chapter.

(NOTE: After this chapter, you may want to turn to page 171 and read "Erica's Story," a testimony by a young girl who was baptized in the Spirit.)

NINE

The Gift of the Spirit

W HEN THE HOLY SPIRIT IS GIVEN TO A PERSON, he makes a
difference. The Holy Spirit brings a new kind of life—
the life of God in Jesus Christ. And that new life shows itself
in many different ways.

HOW THE SPIRIT WORKS IN US

Jesus said that the Spirit, like the wind, "blows where he
will." Men can't control the Holy Spirit. He goes where he
wants to, when he wants to. But the Holy Spirit is not
aimless. He always seeks to glorify God and he does that by
working in us and through us. Here are some of the ways he
works in us.

**1. The Holy Spirit helps us to know and understand the love
that God has for us personally.** In the letter to the Romans,
Paul says, "God has poured out his love into our hearts by
the Holy Spirit, whom he has given us" (Romans 5:5).

Did you know that if a baby is never touched by human
hands, never held, never sung to, never loved, it will simply
die? Even if the baby is kept warm, and gets enough milk to

drink, and has it's physical needs met. Human beings need love to live.

God pours his love into our hearts by the Holy Spirit. Then we know that he loves us. Then we believe that he loves us.

Sometimes, when people are filled with the Holy Spirit, they have sensations of God's love. They may feel unusually calm and peaceful, like the water on a lake when there are no waves or wind. They may feel very safe, as if they were surrounded by mighty angels. They may feel warm inside, or feel a slight shiver go over their body.

They may feel like laughing or even crying. You may have noticed that sometimes people cry when they are very happy.

I'm a basketball fan and since I grew up in Detroit I'm a Detroit Pistons fan. When the Pistons won the world championship game, the camera showed Isiah Thomas, the Pistons' star player, sitting on the bench with a towel over his face, crying.

You can bet those were tears of relief and joy, not sadness. Sometimes people will cry like that when they experience the love of God poured into their hearts by the Holy Spirit.

I don't know anyone who has these sensations all of the time. But I do know many people who have felt these things from time to time—often during a time of prayer or worship, when the Holy Spirit is being poured out in a special way. These feelings connected to God's love being poured out in our hearts through the Spirit are very special, and very real. But they are not the most important thing about God's love.

We can know God's love for us, even if we never, or only rarely, have these feelings. If you have a father or a mother or a special person in your life who really loves you, you probably don't have feelings of that love all the time. But you know the love is there. And it makes a difference for you. That love makes you stronger and it helps you to live. The Holy Spirit helps us to know God's love in that way too.

When I was first prayed with to be filled with the Holy Spirit, I began to pray the Lord's Prayer. You know how it goes, "Our Father in heaven, hallowed be your name . . ." Earlier I shared how, for many years, I had prayed that prayer just before falling asleep. I prayed it silently, as fast as I could. But as the Holy Spirit came on me, I prayed with a much deeper understanding.

Suddenly, I understood that God really was my Father, that he was right there, receiving my prayer—that he was with me and that he loved me. That was something new for me. It was the Holy Spirit, pouring the love of God into my heart.

2. The Holy Spirit helps us to praise God in some new ways. The Holy Spirit is very interested in helping people to praise and worship God. He gives us a desire to praise God. He inspires us to praise God. And he helps us to praise God.

One of the most unusual and interesting ways he does this is by giving people the ability to praise God in a language they don't understand, but which God does. This special praise language is called "tongues," or "the gift of tongues." *Tongue,* as used here, is just another word for language.

I'll tell you what it was like for me when God gave me this ability to praise him with a special language. I used to sit in my living room and try to do what the Bible spoke about so much—praise God. I had praised God in a church service, and that was good. But I wanted to praise him more than that. So I sat down and tried to do it. I said, "Praise you God . . . You are so great . . . I praise you." Well, you know what happened. I ran out of things to say after about three sentences. I thought to myself, "I definitely need some more help than this to praise God the way I want to."

Sometime later, some people prayed with me to be filled with the Holy Spirit. While they were praying, I asked God to give me the gift of tongues. After a few minutes, I stopped praying aloud in English, but kept praying—only it was in a language I didn't understand. I didn't have to think a lot about what I was saying. I knew that I was praising God with the help of the Holy Spirit, and that God understood my praises. It was a very enjoyable experience, something I've done many times since as a way of worshiping God.

Now, if you are like me, you probably have several questions about this gift. Let me see if I can guess what two of your questions might be.

Q: What kind of language does a person speak, when he speaks in tongues? St. Paul referred to "the tongues of men and angels." Some praise languages are known languages, spoken somewhere in the world.

I have a friend from the southern tip of India. Many people in his church pray in tongues. He once invited a friend of his who was from Ethiopia, a country in Africa, to attend his church service. This Ethiopian was not a Christian. During a time of worship one of the church members seated next to the Ethiopian was praying in an unknown language. The Ethiopian visitor was completely astonished. He turned to my friend Joseph and said, "This man next to me is praying in my language!"

Joseph said, "What is he saying in your language?"

"He's speaking out various praises to God. But he looks like an Indian. Could he know my language?"

Joseph said, "Of course not. He's a peasant here and only

knows one language, Malayalam."

The Ethiopian was extremely impressed, and soon became a Christian.

I know another visitor to a local Lutheran church, where many of the people were praising God in other tongues. For some reason, he knew an old form of an unusual language. I think it was a language spoken in Iceland many years ago, but not currently. Naturally, the person praising God in this unknown language had no idea that he was speaking Old Icelandic, but he was!

There are so many languages around the world, and there have been many which are no longer used anywhere. Apparently God likes to be praised in all of these languages.

It is also quite possible that some unknown tongues are not human languages at all, either past or present. They may be "heavenly languages." Paul refers to them as the "tongues of angels." These are languages which God alone understands.

Q: What is it like when you are speaking in tongues? Does God just take over your mouth and force you to do it? I know some people have reported times when it seemed they could hardly keep themselves from speaking in tongues, or for that matter hardly stop once they started! One man I know turned to Jesus, asked to be filled with the Spirit and experienced what felt to him like a bolt of electricity go through his body. Without even knowing what was happening, he began to pray in tongues. That kind of experience is possible, but it is not normally what it is like to pray in tongues!

On the day of Pentecost, when the Spirit was first poured out, the Bible says, "All of them were filled with the Spirit and began to speak in tongues as the Spirit enabled them."

When you speak in tongues, you begin to speak—that is,

you breathe in, push the air past your voice box, and move your mouth as you normally do when you speak. As you speak out, the Holy Spirit gives form to the words you are speaking.

It's not likely that you will speak in tongues if you sit with your arms folded, your teeth clenched, waiting for the Holy Spirit to force you to speak. Instead, you begin to speak, and as you do, the Holy Spirit enables you to pray in an unknown tongue. So you don't have to worry about speaking in tongues as you walk through the halls at school, without wanting to. It doesn't work like that. You have to be willing to speak in tongues. You do the speaking and the Holy Spirit shapes the language.

3. The Holy Spirit can make you God's instrument to do the work of his Son Jesus in the world. After the Holy Spirit was poured out on the day of Pentecost, the disciples had a new power. They told others of the good news and many came to believe in Jesus. They prayed with the sick, and some were dramatically healed. They helped people who were in need of God's love: children without any parents, people who were hungry and homeless, people who were in prison or very troubled, and many ordinary people who just needed to know that God exists, that he has sent his Son Jesus into the world to forgive our sins.

Did you know that the Holy Spirit can work through you to bring the love of Jesus to others?

John Wimber, a pastor who teaches others how to pray for healing, was giving a conference on healing that I attended. During one of the sessions, he felt that God wanted to do some physical healing. He asked the youngest members of the crowd to volunteer to lay hands on the sick in front of everyone to demonstrate that you don't have to be an expert in order for God to work through you.

Five or six courageous young people—I would guess junior high students—came forward. Pastor Wimber called forward a number of individuals whom he felt, by revelation, the Lord wanted to heal. Each person who had some physical pain from arthritis or an old injury, found that the pain went away when the young people prayed with them. Backs that were crooked with a spinal disorder straightened out through prayer.

I've seen young people bring the love of God to others in many different ways—through prayers for healing, through a prophetic message, through visiting lonely elderly people in a nursing home, or through picketing at a local abortion clinic to appeal for the life of unborn babies. I know children who have spoken to relatives and friends about knowing Jesus.

I have never seen God force a young person to do something that was embarrassing or made him feel foolish. But he does, at times, move in your heart to bring the love of Jesus to others.

There are many, many different ways this can happen. Some are more dramatic than others. It's not often something that you carefully plan to do. Often the Holy Spirit gives you a desire to do something, and then puts the words in your mouth or the thoughts in your mind. Sometimes he can work through you without your even knowing it.

4. The Holy Spirit can give you the power to overcome sin and become more like Jesus. You've probably noticed by now that there is something inside of you that likes to sin. It's not enough to know what's right and wrong. Sometimes you know that something is wrong, that it is displeasing to God, but you don't really care. Or if you do care, you feel like you "can't help it."

—Maybe for you it's lying.
—Or being mean to your brother.
—Or stealing "just a few things."
—Or cussing up a storm when you are away from home.
—Or cheating at school.
—Or something more serious than all the things I've mentioned. (Maybe you're feeling a little guilty about it right now. You're hoping I won't mention it!)

Sometimes you can't help it. Sometimes just trying hard not to sin doesn't work. You need help not to sin, more help than a teacher or your parents or anyone else can give you. You need the power of God, the power of the Spirit to help you overcome sin.

The Holy Spirit can give you real power to do what is pleasing to God. If you're not aware that something is wrong, or why it is, or if you "just don't care," the Holy Spirit can make it clear. It's much more effective than just hearing someone say, "Don't do this . . . don't do that."

The Holy Spirit can convince you so that you really want to avoid sin and do what is right, not just so you won't get caught, but because now you really want to do what pleases God.

The Holy Spirit can also just flat out help you. Let's say you've been falling into the bad habit of lying. If you want to be more like Jesus (a desire the Holy Spirit can give you) you can simply pray, "Lord help me to speak the truth . . . I can't do it by myself, help me today."

He will help you. You will find it easier to tell the truth. If you fall down, ask him again for help and he'll pick you back up. It's more than just trying harder. It's counting on the power of God to help you.

So what do you think? Do you want the gift of the Holy Spirit? Do you want more of God's power in your life? He's already at work in your life. You couldn't say, "Jesus is Lord"—and mean it—without the Holy Spirit moving in you.

But do you want more of the power of Jesus? It's free for the asking. And if you're ready to ask, God is ready to give you more of his power.

(NOTE: After this chapter you may want to turn to page 175 and read "Maraed's Story," a testimony about how God surprised an angry young girl.)

TEN

Come Near

Come near to God and he will come near to you.
James 4:7

A RE YOU READY to take a few simple but very important
steps toward God?

On July 20, 1969, hundreds of millions of people around
the world had their eyes glued to their television sets as the
first manned spacecraft landed softly on the moon's dusty
surface. Over twenty years later, it doesn't seem so extraordinary, but for those watching it happen for the first time it
was an historic moment, full of drama and excitement. The
television camera showed the legs of astronaut Neil
Armstrong as he climbed out of the spacecraft and took a
few steps down a metal ladder. Just before he stepped onto
the moon's surface he said, "That's one small step for [a]
man, one giant leap for mankind." How many steps had he
taken in his lifetime? This *was* just another step ... but it was
a very important step.

Picture a young girl playing out in an open field on a
windy day. She comes dangerously close to the edge of the
field, which is a cliff dropping straight down into a rocky
ravine. The sight of the drop-off makes the little girl dizzy

with fright. She does what many of us do when frightened: she stops dead in her tracks as if paralyzed.

The girl's mother sees her from a distance and calls out, "Laura! Come back!" Laura replies, "I'm scared!" Laura's mom is scared too, because the wind could blow her daughter off at any time. "Just take one step toward me, Laura. You can do that—just one step."

STEPS TOWARD GOD

Taking a step is not a very difficult thing to do, but even a few steps can make a world of difference. Steps toward God are steps like that.

Step One: Say "No!" to Satan and his ways. Imagine what it would be like to know someone who is truly evil. This person is cruel to animals for no reason. He loves to see people suffer. He wouldn't hesitate to kill someone if he thought he could get away with it. He is a crafty liar.

Now imagine that this person is trying to pretend to be your friend. He calls you up on the phone to talk, invites himself over to visit. He can put on a great act, too. At times he seems like the nicest person in the world, great fun and very interesting. He always seems to have the latest gadgets to fool around with and plenty of spare cash, and at first he shares all these things with you.

But the more you hang around with him, the farther you go away from God. You begin to lie and to cheat. All in good fun at first, of course. Then you start stealing little things— again, all "just for kicks." The more you hang out with this person the more doubts you have about God.

Satan is something like this so called "friend." He is a

personal influence toward evil, seeking to capture people for hell, seeking to drive them away from God.

"Resist the devil, and he will flee from you. Come near to God and he will come near to you" (James 4:7-8). In order to come near to God you need to say "No" loud and clear to the kingdom of darkness. You can do this with the help of Jesus, who has power over the work of the devil. It is called renouncing Satan and it simply means saying, "I don't want to have *anything* to do with the devil or his way of doing things. I renounce Satan and all wrongdoing in the name of Jesus."

Step Two: Say "Yes!" to Jesus. "The tongue has the power of life and death" (Proverbs 18:21). It is easy to think that words don't really have any real power. But some words have a great deal of power. In the eyes of God, words are very powerful.

Think of it! God made the heavens and the earth by speaking a few powerful words: "Let there be light!" Jesus raised his friend Lazarus from the dead with a few powerful words: "Lazarus come out!"

God's word says, "If you confess with your mouth, 'Jesus is Lord,' and believe in your heart that God raised him from the dead, you will be saved" (Romans 10:9).

You can take an important step toward God by speaking aloud your belief in Jesus as the Son of God, risen from the dead. Don't just think it, don't just mumble it to yourself with no one around, but say it loud and clear.

Such a clear statement can be even stronger if you say it in the presence of some other people. You know from experience that if you say something that others hear, somehow there is "more to it."

Whenever people make a solemn promise they say it in

the presence of others who are called "witnesses." When a man and woman get married, they make their marriage promises in front of at least two witnesses. If a person is called to tell certain facts in a courtroom to a judge, he speaks before others who are witnesses to what is said.

So if you want to make your confession, your words of belief in Jesus, with some "oomph"—so that it makes a real difference—look for an opportunity to speak out in the presence of some other people. Or tell someone what you have said to the Lord. When you are ready, you can say something like this,

> Lord Jesus, I believe that you are the Lord. You are the Son of God. You died for my sins, and you were raised from the dead to give me new life. I believe in you, and I want to serve you, follow you, and obey you.

Step Three: Ask Jesus to baptize or fill you with the Holy Spirit. Chances are, you already believe in Jesus. You are a Christian. You may have been baptized in water as a baby. Perhaps you have learned about Jesus from the time you were a young child.

Already, the Holy Spirit has been at work in you. The Bible says that no one can say, "Jesus is Lord" except by the Holy Spirit. If you believe in Jesus, it is because the Holy Spirit has been at work in you. But there is a lot more power from the Holy Spirit available to you.

Imagine an empty glass. It's large, clean, and clear. Now think about pouring a small thimble full of your favorite drink into that large glass—water, chocolate milk, juice, Coke—whatever it is that you like best, and at just the right temperature. Now if you have a large glass with a small amount of your favorite drink sitting at the bottom of the glass, your next thought is probably "Fill it up!"

Your heart is like the large glass. And your favorite drink is like the Holy Spirit. Wouldn't you like to have your heart filled with the Holy Spirit? There's only one thing you have to do. In fact there's only one thing you *can* do. Ask!

Perhaps you are a little bit reluctant to ask for the Holy Spirit. Jesus has some encouraging words for you:

> I say to you: Ask and it will be given to you . . . for everyone who asks receives. . . . Which of you fathers, if your son asks for a fish, will give him a snake instead? Or if he asks for an egg, will give him a scorpion? If you then, though you are evil, know how to give good gifts to your children, how much more will your Father in heaven give the Holy Spirit to those who ask him! Luke 11:9-13

So when you are ready, simply ask, "Lord, I ask you to baptize me, to fill me with the Holy Spirit. Come, Holy Spirit, and fill my heart."

When you ask to be baptized or filled with the Spirit, I would suggest that you also ask for the gift of tongues. "Lord, fill me with the Holy Spirit and give me the gift of tongues."

Why would I suggest that you do this? Let me tell you a few reasons.

In the Book of Acts, the story of the first Christians, whenever people were baptized in the Holy Spirit, it appears that they were also given a new ability to praise God, usually in tongues. I think this prayer language is something the Lord is willing to give very freely to those who ask (and to some who don't ask!)

The gift of tongues is by no means the most important gift of the Spirit. In fact, the Bible says it is the least of the gifts.

But it is often the first gift of the Spirit that people are given. And some would say receiving the gift of tongues helps us to be more open to other, more important, gifts.

Of course, if you don't want to speak in tongues, you don't have to. But the gift of tongues will help you to praise God, so why not ask?

If you do ask for this gift, simply take some time to pray out loud in English. You can use simple phrases for praise used in the Bible, "Praise to you Lord ... Hallelujah ... glory to you, Jesus." Then stop using English words, but keep praying, speaking out the words in tongues that the Holy Spirit gives you. Don't worry about what you are saying, or how it sounds. Just speak out your prayer in tongues to the Lord and keep your mind on him.

LETTING THE SPIRIT WORK

Here are a few simple suggestions to keep in mind when you are prayed with:

1. Relax. Sometimes people get all worked up inside over the thought of receiving the Holy Spirit. They may get nervous or tense because they think they have to do something "just right" in order for God to pour out his Spirit on them. Not true. If that were the case, no one would be filled with the Spirit. As it is, God is pouring out his Spirit all over the world on many, many people. Not because they are "doing it right," but only because he wants to and he's prompted them to ask.

So relax, because asking is all you can do. And it is not difficult to do.

Sometimes people get tense because they are afraid that

when God pours out his Spirit, he will force them to do something that would be embarrassing. Not to worry. The Holy Spirit is not interested in making a fool out of you. Whatever he does in you will be good.

2. Pray out loud. When it is time to pray, pray out loud—at least sometime. Just speak in a normal tone of voice. There's no need to yell (though shouting your praise is fine at times).

At times we pray silently, the words in our minds and hearts, not spoken out. But when it is time to take those important steps toward God referred to earlier, speak up.

When you ask for the gift of tongues, there is another reason to pray out loud. It's a little bit like steering a car. A car that is not moving at all is very difficult to steer. The steering wheel won't budge. There's too much friction. But once the car is rolling, even a little, it is much easier to steer. Praying aloud is like getting the car rolling so that the Holy Spirit can direct your speaking.

3. Don't worry about what you are feeling. When the Spirit of God comes on you, you may feel any number of different things. You may feel like smiling or laughing. Go ahead. You may feel like crying. You don't have to, but why not?

You may feel very peaceful and still inside. You may feel a warm sensation. Your body may feel heavy. You may feel a tingling sensation on your face or hands or some other part of your body. Perhaps you will experience something that you just cannot put into words.

These are very common feelings. But it is also common to feel nothing in particular. That doesn't mean the Holy Spirit is not working. It just means you are not feeling anything in particular.

Whether you have strong feelings of one kind or another,

mild sensations, or nothing at all, is not the point. The Holy Spirit wants to make God's love known to you. He wants to show you that your sins are forgiven, that you really do belong to God. He wants to give you a new power to live the life of Jesus.

PRAYERS FOR DRAWING NEAR

The following prayers can be used when you are ready to take some steps toward the Lord. Begin by stating your faith in Jesus. After each question, speak out your response.

Question: Do you renounce Satan and all works of evil?

Suggested Response: Yes, I renounce Satan and all works of evil in the name of Jesus Christ.

Question: Do you believe that Jesus is the Son of God?

Suggested Response: Yes, I believe that Jesus is the Son of God. I believe that he died to free me from my sins and that he rose again to give me a new life.

Question: Do you choose to follow Jesus as your Lord?

Suggested Response: Yes, I want to follow Jesus as my Lord. I want to love him, honor him, and obey him.

Prayer for the gift of the Spirit:

Father, I ask you to baptize me in the Holy Spirit. Fill me with your Spirit and help me to worship you in Spirit and in truth. I ask you to give me the gift of tongues and any other gifts you wish to give me. I ask this in the name of Jesus. Amen.

ELEVEN

The Kingdom Seed

I F YOU ARE ALIVE, you are growing. Maybe you are growing slowly. Or maybe you are in a growth spurt—and the grocery bill is increasing every month.

Have you ever stopped to ask yourself why or how you are growing? Probably not. You're just growing, without thinking about it. But think about it for a minute. How is it that you are growing?

GROWTH IS NATURAL

It's not as if you *decided* to grow: "I'd like to be taller. I think I'll grow three inches this month."

Or that you are trying to grow. "Come on, body, grow! Taller! Stronger! Get moving!" I used to think up all sorts of different schemes for getting taller faster, usually on my way to sleep at night. I would imagine a machine that could stretch my body out. I wondered if hanging upside down would help. I never tried the machine, and the hanging upside down didn't help!

When it gets right down to it, you are growing because God gave you life. Once your life began in your mother's womb, you began to grow—without deciding to grow and without trying to grow.

While you cannot make yourself grow, you can hinder the growing process. For example, if you stopped eating, sooner or later you would stop growing! If you turned into a "couch potato"—your only exercise being those trips to the refrigerator during commercials—your muscles wouldn't grow the way they are supposed to grow.

And, of course, you can do some things which allow you to grow—eating the right foods, exercising, avoiding low flying airplanes.

Much the same is true for growing in the life of Christ. When all is said and done, you cannot make yourself grow: "Neither he who plants nor he who waters is anything, but only God, who makes things grow" (1 Corinthians 3:7). To grow physically means to get taller and stronger. To grow spiritually means becoming more like Jesus—more full of love, more kind, more of a servant toward others, more joyful, more courageous, more obedient to God.

You cannot make yourself grow in Christ, but you can help or hinder the growth that God gives. You can do some things which slow or even stop the growth God wants to give. And you can allow God's life to grow within you.

GROWTH ACCORDING TO JESUS

Jesus told a story about a farmer who went out to plant some seed. Some of the seed fell on a hard, dried-out dirt path. The birds came by and ate the seed. Other seed fell on rocky soil without much dirt. The seeds took root quickly, but died. Other seed fell among thorny bushes that choked out the newly forming plants. Only the seed that fell into good, rich soil grew and produced a large crop.

This story tells a great deal about growing as a disciple of Jesus. Jesus explained what he meant by the story: "The farmer sows the word" (Mark 4:14).

The seed stands for the word of God. Life and growth comes from God's word.

Think for a moment. What could you do to receive God's word in order to grow? Where could you go to hear God's word? Where could you find God's word? How could you receive God's word every day? How could you understand God's word so that it made sense to you? I think you will come up with some pretty good ideas, if you stop to think about it.

GOD'S ENEMY (AND YOURS)

"Some people are like seed along the path.... As soon as they hear it, Satan comes and takes away the word that was sown in them" (Mark 4:15).

In the Bible, birds often stand for the work of Satan. I was once visiting my grandmother, who had white hair that was tinted slightly blue. (This used to be the fashion for older women.) One morning she was standing in her backyard hanging some clothes on the clothesline. A large blue jay circled over her and then dove at her hair and began to peck at my poor grandmother's head! So birds as a symbol of Satan's work make perfect sense to me.

Jesus said that the bird who ate the seed along the path stood for Satan, who likes to rob us of the seed of God's word once we have heard it. In other words, we have a spiritual enemy who doesn't want us to hear or to hold onto God's word.

Can you imagine how a spiritual enemy might try to rob you of God's word? Perhaps he would try to "suggest" to you that God's word is not true, or that you could not possibly understand it or obey it. Perhaps he would try to make you forget God's word or get your mind distracted while God is trying to speak his word to you.

Satan has a thousand and one tricks, so it is good to beware that his tactics don't fool you.

PERSEVERE WHEN IT'S HARD

"Others, like seed sown on rocky places, hear the word and at once receive it with joy. But since they have no root, they last only a short time. When trouble or persecution comes because of the word, they quickly fall away" (Mark 4:16-17).

Sometimes people think that because they are Christians they shouldn't have any problems—life should be smooth and trouble free. But Jesus told his disciples that "in this world, you will have troubles."

You know—troubles: students at school who harass you, a misunderstanding with a friend, someone in your family gets seriously sick or dies. You get twenty dollars from your favorite uncle for your birthday and someone throws the card (and the cash) away by mistake. You get a notice from the public library informing you that you have ten books that are a year overdue... if you begin working now, you can repay the debt in twenty years! Your dog gets hit by a car. You do something that you feel terribly ashamed of and it doesn't seem like there is anyone who will understand. Your father loses his job.

The troubles we face in life can do one of two things. They can either drive us away from God (because we get mad at

God, or discouraged, or preoccupied with our problems) or they can bring us closer to God. God wants to be with us in our troubles. Sometimes, he takes the trouble away. Sometimes he gives us the wisdom or the strength to endure the trouble. But always, he wants to be with us.

My daughter, Maja (pronounced Maya), was feeling pressured about schoolwork recently. (Maja is in high school—big time!) She had to miss a lot of school this past semester because she injured her knee, so she didn't feel ready for her final exams.

She had to make up an English exam, but she didn't feel prepared. The night before the test, she prayed, "Oh Lord, I'm not ready for this . . . please let the teacher be absent so I can take it later."

That morning she saw the English teacher in the hallway. "Oh well!" she thought. But when she arrived after school to make up her test, the teacher said, "Maja! I'm so sorry. I forgot you were supposed to take your test today. Is it OK with you if we wait until tomorrow?"

That time, the Lord helped Maja by changing the circumstances. But she still had to take the rest of her final exams, even though she didn't feel prepared. At times, she probably felt anxious and pressured, but God gave her the strength to make it through all of her exams.

The power of the Holy Spirit isn't given just to take away our problems, but his power is there for us to go through our problems with his help. He gives us a new power to help us deal with our problems.

FACE UP TO OPPOSITION

Jesus also said that persecution—harassment from others that comes because you are a Christian—can keep us from holding onto his word, and therefore from growing spiritually. For example, in some places, it is actually against the law to be a Christian. If the government of such a country finds out that you are a believer in Jesus, you might be thrown in jail—or worse. Under that kind of pressure, some Christians have denied their faith.

Right now, you are probably not facing that kind of persecution. But there are small ways that other people can pressure you because you are a Christian. For example, perhaps there are certain kinds of music that you refuse to listen to because the musicians mock God or glorify Satan. A few of your friends don't see it the same way, and when they find out what you think, they make fun of you. "This music is great, what's wrong with you?"

When other people around you think it is stupid to be a Christian, to obey God's commands, to believe in Jesus, it can make you timid about standing up for your faith. You may want to keep your faith in Jesus a secret. At times, you might be tempted to wish you weren't a Christian.

If we give in to this pressure from others, you can see how it will keep us from growing in the life of the Spirit. Sometimes we have to be ready to take a little flack, because we believe in Jesus and want to follow him.

TOO BUSY FOR GOD?

"Still others, like seed sown among thorns, hear the word; but the worries of this life, the deceitfulness of wealth and the desires for other things come in and choke the word" (Mark 4:18-19).

Perhaps you know what it's like when your parents are very busy and don't seem to have much time for you. Maybe you don't feel very close to them; it might be easy to feel angry or misunderstood. Sometimes we can get too busy for God. We can get so involved in other things, that there just doesn't seem to be time for God: no time to pray, no time to read the Bible, no time to go to church. When that happens, the growth that comes through God's word in us can get choked off.

Sometimes we can get involved with things that draw us away from God. For example, if I watch long hours of television, I find that I'm just not that interested in God. God seems far off, distant, boring, bothersome.

A man once conducted an experiment with monkeys. He built a large wood box around a coconut. He cut a hole in the box large enough for a monkey's hand, but too small for the coconut to be removed. Naturally, upon finding this box, the monkey will put his hand through the hole and grab the coconut. Monkeys are very fond of coconuts. And sometimes a monkey will want that coconut so badly that he just won't let go of it, even though he can't pull it out of the box to eat it. He will actually refuse to take hold of good food that he can eat, because he doesn't want to let the coconut go.

Sometimes we have to let go of things we want—even things that are not bad in themselves, in order to take hold of what God has for us. How will you know whether to let go of something or not? You will know. The Holy Spirit will gently nudge you.

NURTURING LIFE IN GOD

"Others, like seed sown on good soil, hear the word, accept it, and produce a crop—thirty, sixty, or even a hundred times what was sown" (Mark 4:20).

The most important thing you can do to allow the life of Christ to grow in you, to become more like Jesus, is to hear God's word and accept it.

What does that mean for you?

- Maybe it means that you hear that God loves you and you accept the fact that he loves you.

- Perhaps it means that you hear God's word of forgiveness from Jesus and you accept his forgiveness for your sins.

- Or you hear his word of command to love your fellow man and you accept that word and ask him to help you love that person in school that no one likes, or you decide to help someone in your family.

- Perhaps it means that you come to God with humility. This means you realize that God is bigger, smarter, and wiser than you are, that you need God's help, and that he knows what is best for you.

As you do this, as you hear and accept God's word, good things will happen. You will grow. You will become more like Jesus. God will use you to help others and to show them his love.

ONLY THE BEGINNING

I was at a prayer meeting attended largely by high school students in a troubled section of a major city. Many of the young people there had grown up with gang violence, alcoholism, drugs, and poverty. No one was putting on a show or trying to look good. A young man prayed out a simple prayer that expressed a deep truth: "Lord, thank you that there's always something new and fresh to discover about you. You don't get stale. You're always ready to show us something we didn't expect. It's good to know you. It's exciting to find out who you are and what you can do in us. There's no end to you." There's more. This is one of the most exciting things about learning to know God in Jesus Christ. You can't ever reach the end of his goodness. There's always more. Once you think you really know what his love is all about, be sure of this—you've only scratched the surface. There's more. Once you think you've learned all there is to know about him, you will discover something new and amazing that will surprise you again.

So the end of this book isn't really an ending at all. It's a beginning—the beginning of the adventure called knowing Jesus Christ.

PART THREE

Daily Meditations:
For Those Who Want to Set Aside Daily Time with Jesus

Introduction

IF YOU ARE PRESENTING THIS MATERIAL to several young people at a time, each should have his or her own copy of this next section (from pp. 119-176). The publisher has given permission to make up to five copies of the Daily Meditations for each book purchased.

If you need more than five copies, please send your request to:

Servant Publications
P.O. Box 8617
Ann Arbor, MI 48107

The following meditations can be used with this book in two different ways.

1. After the book is completed, provide twenty-five meditations to review the content of Part Two.

2. If you are reading one chapter a week from Part Two, use the meditations on the days between chapters. Meditations one to five following chapter six, "God's Love"; six to ten following chapter seven, "What's Wrong?"; eleven to fifteen following chapter eight, "Knowing God"; sixteen to twenty following chapter nine, "The Gift of the Spirit"; and twenty-one to twenty-five following chapter ten, "Come Near."

No meditation follows the final chapter, "The Kingdom Seed."

ONE

The Gift

For God so loved the world that he gave his one and only Son, that whoever believes in him shall not perish but have eternal life. John 3:16

HOW DO YOU KNOW THAT someone really loves you?

When a person smiles at you or says something nice to you, That's a start, but a good salesman will do as much when he's hoping to sell you something.

"For God so loved the world that *he gave* . . ."

You know someone really loves you when he is willing to give you something that costs him dearly.

A young boy went to the hospital with his parents to visit his sister who was very sick. A doctor came into the room and asked to speak privately to his mom and dad. When they came back, they looked pretty grim. The boy's father told him that his sister needed a blood transfusion to get better.

"There's only one problem," his father said. "Your sister has a very rare blood type, different from mine and your mother's. It's so rare that the hospital doesn't have any. It's the same blood type that you have, so the doctors would like to take a pint of your blood and give it to your sister. Would you be willing to do that?"

The boy swallowed hard. He didn't like the sight of blood, especially when it was leaving his body. But he looked at his sister, and knew that she needed help. "Sure Dad," the boy said, trying to hide his fear, "No problem."

A few minutes later someone arrived to take the young boy's blood. When it was all over, the boy had a puzzled look, so his mother asked him what was on his mind.

"Oh nothing," he said, "I just thought you needed your blood to live."

"Of course you do," the boy's mother replied.

"So how come I'm not dead yet?"

The young man thought that his sister needed *all* of his blood. When he said "yes" to his father's request, he thought he was giving his life.

Suggested Prayer: "Lord, thank you for giving me your one and only Son, as a sign of your love for me."

TWO

Friends

My command is this: Love each other as I have loved you. Greater love has no man than this, that one lay down his life for his friends. You are my friends if you do what I command. I no longer call you servants, because a servant does not know his master's business. Instead, I have called you friends, for everything that I learned from my Father I have made known to you. **John 15:12-15**

JESUS COMES WITH AN AMAZING MESSAGE from heaven: we can be friends with God, by knowing Jesus. We've heard that before, but it is pretty amazing. Jesus wants us as friends.

Compared to God, we are insignificant, puny—tiny dots in a huge universe. Consider that there are four billion people alive on the earth. McDonald's has sold sixty billion hamburgers. That makes a lot of people and a lot of burgers!

To us, the earth seems fairly big. Walking or swimming around the earth is not something you plan to do on your summer vacation. But you can fit a million earths into the sun. And compared to all the other stars in the universe, the sun—so much larger than the earth—is like a single grain of sand on a very large beach.

How many stars are there, besides our sun? There are

100,000,000,000,000,000,000 (more or less). If you think you can imagine how many that really is, forget it.

It took a great and awesome God to create this universe. Even though we are a very small part of it, this God wants to be friends with us. He sent his one and only Son as an offer of friendship. And that Son was the one who said to us, "I have called you friends."

Suggested Prayer: "Lord, show me what it means to be your friend. Reveal yourself to me."

THREE

Power to Live

I have come that they may have life, and have it to the full. John 10:10

APART FROM JESUS, we are like a portable radio with no battery. Such a contraption looks like a radio, has an on-off switch, dial, speaker, and a volume control, but doesn't work. There's no sound, no music, no weather forecast, no Ernie Harwell. (Sorry if you don't know who Ernie Harwell is, but he's my favorite sportscaster.)

In order to live the kind of life that God created us to live, we need power to live. We need something or someone to energize us, to make us really alive.

Why did Jesus come? To give us life. Not just a little life, not like a radio with a weak battery, so that you can barely hear the music, but "life to the full." Abundant life. Overflowing life. A better life than we could ever imagine. So that we can do more, and be more than we ever thought possible.

I came that they may have life, and have it to the full.

Suggested Prayer: "Jesus, you are the one who came to give us life. I want your power to live an abundant life."

FOUR

Anybody Home?

Anyone who comes to him must believe that he exists and that he rewards those who earnestly seek him.

Hebrews 11:6

COMING CLOSER TO GOD isn't complicated or difficult. It just takes believing that he exists and that he makes it worth your while to seek him.

Imagine you're walking over to a friend's house, but as you approach, the house looks empty. There's no car in the driveway, no lights are visible, and the curtains are closed. So you hesitate, thinking "Ahh, there's probably no one home. What's the use?" You turn around and begin to walk away.

Then you realize how boring it will be to spend the afternoon alone. You take another look in the direction of your friend's house. It looks the same, but this time you notice that the front door is slightly open. Why would the door be ajar, if nobody was home? When you hear your friend's voice saying, "Come on in!" you are glad that you bothered to look back, after all.

Anyone who comes to him, must believe that he exists and that he rewards those who earnestly seek him.

Suggested Prayer: "Lord, though you are invisible, I believe that you exist and that you will reward those who seek you. Help me to earnestly seek you."

FIVE

Ask!

So I say to you: Ask and it will be given to you; seek and you will find; knock and the door will be opened to you. For everyone who asks receives; he who seeks finds; and to him who knocks, the door will be opened.

Which of you fathers, if your son asks for a fish, will give him a snake instead? Or if he asks for an egg, will give him a scorpion? If you then, though you are evil, know how to give good gifts to your children, how much more will your Father in heaven give the Holy Spirit to those who ask him! **Luke 11:9-13**

THIS IS ONE OF THE MOST IMPORTANT passages to remember from the entire Bible.

Who receives the Holy Spirit? A few people who are very clever? The unusual person who is especially religious?

No. "Everyone *who asks* receives."

Not "most everyone."

Not "practically everyone."

Not "everyone except . . ."

Everyone who asks.

Suggested Prayer: "Father in heaven, I thank you for this promise: everyone who asks receives."

SIX

The Mess We're In

The Lord saw how great man's wickedness on the earth had become, and that every inclination of the thoughts of his heart was only evil all the time. The Lord was grieved that he had made man on the earth, and his heart was filled with pain. **Genesis 6:5-6**

PETER PAN HAD an interesting approach to life. His motto was, "I won't grow up." It worked for Peter Pan—he didn't grow up. But we don't have the option.

And as we grow up, we begin to notice that things don't work out like they do in the cartoons or the storybooks. We begin to notice that something is seriously wrong with the world we live in. It's easy to point out where the problems are:

- People get sick.
- Some people are rich while others sleep on the streets.
- Parents fight with each other.
- Things aren't fair.
- There always seems to be a war going on somewhere.
- People hate each other for crazy reasons.
- Smart people do stupid things, like using illegal drugs, or drinking too much alcohol.
- Oh yes,—all living things eventually die.

Some people think we can just fix all these problems ourselves with enough time, enough money, enough hard work. What do you think?

The Bible says that we are facing a problem too big for us to solve alone. We are in over our heads. We need God to save us from the mess we've made of things.

Suggested Prayer: "Lord, in spite of all the good things in life, something is very wrong with the whole world. Help me to understand what is wrong and your plan to make it right."

SEVEN

Designed for What?

The First Spiritual Law:
God loves you and has a wonderful plan
for your life.

*"For I know the plans I have for you," declares the
Lord, "plans to prosper you and not to harm you,
plans to give you hope and a future."* **Jeremiah 29:11**

NOT TOO LONG AGO, a primitive tribe was discovered in
Indonesia. They knew as little of our world as we did of
theirs. They knew nothing of electricity, television, phones,
or modern appliances. They had seen planes flying over-
head, but they didn't know that people flew the planes.

Imagine someone from this tribe at your house for a visit.
He's alone in the kitchen, trying to figure out what this
gadget that we call a toaster is for.

At first he thinks it must be a finger warmer. After a quick
trial, he decides that it's better to have cold fingers than to
warm them in a gadget like this.

He once saw someone melting butter for popcorn. Maybe
that's what this thing is for. Soon he realizes that there has
got to be a better way to melt butter for popcorn.

Perhaps this is what these crazy modern people use to
warm up their cold water! The steam, smoke, and sparks tell
him that he has yet to solve the mystery.

What is this man's problem? He may be a genius but he doesn't know what a toaster is designed for.

Like the toaster, you were designed with a special purpose in mind. If you try to do something that you were not created for, it won't work out very well.

We know that God designed you to love and serve him. As time goes on, the specific plan he has for your life will become more clear to you as you seek him.

It's something to think about: the God who made you has a plan for your life. He made you for a reason. He has a plan for you, a wonderful plan.

"I know the plans I have for you," declares the Lord.

Suggested Prayer: "Thank you, God, for creating me for a special purpose. Help me to discover the plan you have for my life."

EIGHT

The Sin Problem

The Second Spiritual Law:
We have been separated from God
and his plan through sin.

For all have sinned and fall short of the glory of God.
Romans 3:23

THE LORD OF THE FLIES, by William Golding, is a book about a group of English school children who are shipwrecked on a deserted island. All the adults were killed in the wreck. Only the students survived.

There were no other people on the island. The children all thought that this was a great chance to "do things right." They could set things up however they wanted things to be. They could create a "heaven on earth." And why not? They were all pretty good kids.

So what happened? Did they create an island paradise with no problems, no crime, with everything peaceful and good?

Everyone was happy at first. But then things started to go wrong. By the end of the story, the children were at war with each other. Not just sticks and stones and name-calling, but a real war. They were killing each other off.

All the things that are wrong with the world can be boiled down to one problem: the sin problem. The students in that story weren't especially bad kids. But they forgot about the sin problem.

There is a double-whammy to the sin problem. It hits us from two sides. On the one hand, sin—lying, cheating, being mean, and all the rest—is simply doing wrong.

On the other hand, sin is like a disease. It's a condition we are all born with. It's passed on from one generation to the next, like babies who are born with AIDS from mothers who have AIDS themselves.

So we choose to do wrong (like when we tell a lie to avoid punishment or to look good). And we are born with the sin-disease, so that all of us have this tendency to sin. Sooner or later, it shows up.

The whole world, including each of us, is facing the sin problem.

Suggested Prayer: "Lord Jesus, save me from the sin problem."

NINE

A Costly Job

The Third Spiritual Law:
Jesus bridges the gap between us and God.

Jesus answered, "I am the way and the truth and the life. No one comes to the Father except through me."
John 14:6

HAVE YOU EVER SEEN THE MACKINAC BRIDGE? It connects the upper and lower parts of the State of Michigan. It's quite a bridge—five miles long.

Can you imagine what a job it is to build a bridge like that? It takes millions of dollars, thousands of workers, and years of labor to build such a massive bridge.

It also costs some people their lives. When the Golden Gate Bridge was built in San Francisco, "only" seven men died while building the bridge. Normally, more workers are killed, but the builders of the Golden Gate Bridge put huge nets under the workers to catch them if they fell. And fall they did, when great gusts of wind blew across the San Francisco Bay.

Building a bridge that long is a costly job. The biggest, most expensive bridge ever built was the bridge between heaven and earth. That bridge doesn't just cross a river, or even a large lake. That bridge crosses all the sin that stands between God and human beings.

God didn't leave us to build the bridge. He had to do it for us. And he did, by sending Jesus, who is the way back to the Father, the way to heaven.

With one firm hand, Jesus holds on to the Father. And with the other he reaches out to us. Jesus is the bridge between heaven and earth. Jesus is the bridge between the righteous Father and sinful human beings, including you and me.

Suggested Prayer: "Thank you, Father, for building a bridge between heaven and earth. Thank you for sending Jesus, who is the way, the truth, and the life."

TEN

Cross Over!

The Fourth Spiritual Law:
We must accept Jesus as our Lord and Savior.

Whoever believes in the Son has eternal life, but whoever rejects the Son will not see life. **John 3:36**

WHAT GOOD IS A BRIDGE, if we don't walk across it?

What good is a present, if we don't accept it and open it?

If a person is close to drowning, and someone throws him a lifeline, does he throw it back because it's not his favorite color?

Believing in Jesus means believing that he is the Son of God, who died for your sins and was raised to life to give you a new life with him.

Believing in Jesus means accepting him; not just accepting the fact that he exists, but accepting the fact that he is the Lord.

It means accepting him as *your* Lord, accepting
That he is in charge of your life.
That he calls the shots.
That you are willing to do things his way.
That you are willing to follow him.

Suggested Prayer: "Lord Jesus, give me the willingness and the desire to follow you."

ELEVEN

The Phone Booth

Suppose one of you has a hundred sheep and loses one of them. Does he not leave the ninety-nine in the open country and go after the lost sheep until he finds it? **Luke 15:4**

GOD WILL SOMETIMES GO TO VERY GREAT LENGTHS to reveal himself to someone in need. He will pursue the lost sheep until he finds him.

A pastor was driving along the highway and decided to stop off at a Dairy Queen. After getting an ice cream, he was walking back to the car. He passed an outdoor phone booth and noticed that the phone was ringing.

It kept ringing for a long time. This caught the pastor's attention. Who would be calling a phone booth number? To satisfy his curiosity, he answered the phone.

"This is the operator speaking. I have a person-to-person call for Pastor Graber."

The pastor who answered the phone was Pastor Graber.

"How can that be?" he replied. "I just got off the highway for an ice cream at this place I've never been before. How would anyone know where I am? Is this Candid Camera?"

"This is *not* Candid Camera," said the operator. "Are you Pastor Graber or not, because I have a call for you."

"Yes, I am, put it through."

What Pastor Graber learned next was something beyond

his wildest dreams. A woman in another city had seen him on television. She was feeling very troubled. In fact she felt that she might kill herself. The woman said, "Oh God, if you're there, help me to talk to Pastor Graber. Maybe he can help me."

Just then a phone number popped into her mind. It wasn't a number that she knew herself. She thought maybe God had given her the number to reach Pastor Graber. So she placed the call through the operator—not knowing where she was calling.

Little did she know that the phone number that popped into her mind was the phone at the phone booth next to the Dairy Queen, where, for the first time in his life, Pastor Graber had just stopped for an ice cream.

Suggested Prayer: "Thank you, Lord, that you are willing to go to great lengths to reveal yourself to us."

TWELVE

One Step at a Time

Your word is a lamp to my feet and a light for my path. **Psalm 119:105**

GOD'S WORD IN THE BIBLE doesn't tell us everything we might like to know. It doesn't tell us what career to pursue, which person to marry, or who will win the next World Series. It doesn't tell us how many small seeds can be found on the outside of a strawberry. (I never had the patience to count them.)

But his word is a "lamp to my feet and a light for my path." In other words, his word gives us the light we need to walk through the darkness, enough direction to live as he wants us to live.

If you find yourself alone in pitch darkness on a twisting, bumpy path, you don't need a searchlight to find your way along the path.

You just need enough light to light up the next step. In fact, a flashlight will do, as long as you shine it a few feet ahead so that you know where to step.

Normally, God doesn't lay out his plan for our lives in one day. God doesn't tell you one day, "I want you to go to college, become a doctor, and then serve the needy in India." His word is a lamp to our feet. He gives us enough light, enough direction so that we can take one step at a time.

Suggested Prayer: "Father, thank you for revealing yourself in your word. Guide my life through your word."

THIRTEEN

It's Who You Know

If God is for us, who can be against us? **Romans 8:31**

I GREW UP IN THE CITY of Detroit.

Next to our high school was a large open field surrounded by what was called "Pitcher Woods"—a large stand of trees. Pitcher Woods had a reputation for being a dangerous place at nighttime, a good place to get robbed, attacked, or beat up.

One evening, I was walking through the open field next to Pitcher Woods with a friend or two. Out of Pitcher Woods a large gang of troublemakers slowly emerged—about twenty-five strong. They were ominously headed our way.

We knew that we were in trouble. We couldn't outrun them. And we couldn't defend ourselves for very long against so many.

Sure enough, the gang surrounded us and began to jostle us—like a cat playing with a mouse. Just when things were beginning to get nasty, the leader of the gang spoke up.

"Wait a minute! That's Wilson! I know him. Leave 'em alone."

By a stroke of good fortune, the leader of the gang was a runner on the high-school cross-country team. I was the captain of the team, and we knew each other. (Though I didn't know about his evening activities!)

On the one hand, I wasn't very happy with what my teammate was doing with his spare time, and my respect for him went way down. But, on the other hand, at the moment, I was happy to be known as his friend. As long as he was for us, the rest of the gang would not turn against us.

We have a friend in Jesus who is powerful, influential, *and* good. With a friend like him, who do we have to be afraid of?

Suggested Prayer: "Lord, thank you for the protection that comes from being friends with you."

FOURTEEN

Niagara Falls

Since the creation of the world God's invisible qualities—his eternal power and divine nature—have been clearly seen, being understood from what has been made. **Romans 1:20**

PERHAPS YOU'VE BEEN fortunate enough to see one of the great natural wonders of the world: Niagara Falls, on the border between the United States and Canada.

When I think of God's "eternal power" as revealed by the creation, I think of Niagara Falls, an immense waterfall. When you see Niagara Falls for the first time, you have an impression of tremendous power, power felt in the strong current of the Niagara River as it surges toward the edge of the falls, or glimpsed in the sight of a huge wall of water plunging headlong over a cliff. The sound of that water can be heard from far away and sounds like continuous rumbling thunder.

What immense power!

And it seems that there is no end to the water pouring over the falls. When you visit the falls, you stand around and watch for an hour or so. Then you go back to your car, drive off to a restaurant and come back a few hours later. The water is still coming, without letting up a bit.

The next morning it's still there—the roar, the spray, and

the wall of water—year after year, lifetime after lifetime. The American Indians stood in wonder at the sight, hundreds, even thousands of years ago. Later, the first explorers from Europe also witnessed this marvelous sight. And long after we are gone, the water will still be pouring over the falls.

It's a picture of "eternal power." It reminds us that the God who created the heavens and the earth is an awesome God, a God of "eternal power."

Suggested Prayer: "Lord God of heaven and earth, you truly are an awesome God—powerful, mighty, with no beginning and no end. Help me, God, to know you through your Son, Jesus Christ."

FIFTEEN

The Rescue

In your distress you called and I rescued you.
Psalm 81:7

I KNOW A YOUNG MAN NAMED JOSHUA. When Joshua was about ten years old, he was out with his aunt and younger brother, Vincent, visiting a museum. They had parked their car on the third floor of a parking structure on a windy day.

Vincent and his cousins ran ahead to the fourth floor of the parking structure. Vincent climbed on top of the wall at the edge of the structure. A strong gust of wind blew him over.

Joshua heard his brother screaming for help. He looked up from the third level and saw him dangling over the edge of the fourth floor wall. Without a moment's hesitation, Joshua took off. He reached Vincent just in time to grab him by the coat before he fell. But his brother's weight and the strong wind were pulling him over as well. Joshua's aunt arrived to pull them both back to safety.

When I talked to Joshua about what had happened, he shrugged it off as no big deal.

"What did you think when you heard Vincent screaming?"

"I didn't think, I just took off after him."

God is like that with us. When we call out to him in our distress—when we are in need or in trouble—he comes to rescue us. That's what it means to say that our God is a Savior.

Suggested Prayer: "Lord, I thank you that you are a God who comes to my rescue when I cry out to you."

SIXTEEN

Midnight Caller

The boy Samuel ministered before the Lord under Eli. In those days the word of the Lord was rare; there were not many visions.

Samuel was lying down in the temple of the Lord. Then the Lord called Samuel.

Samuel answered, "Here I am." And he ran to Eli and said, "Here I am; you called me."

But Eli said, "I did not call; go back and lie down."

1 Samuel 3:1, 3-5

THREE TIMES THE LORD called out to Samuel, and three times Samuel thought it was Eli calling out from the other room. Finally, Eli said, "I'm telling you, I'm not calling you! Go back to sleep . . . maybe it's God speaking to you."

On the fourth try, the Lord got through to Samuel. This time when Samuel heard that voice calling, "Samuel! Samuel!" he replied, "Speak, Lord, for your servant is listening."

Ask yourself a few questions in light of this story.

1. Do you have to wait until you are an adult to know God?

2. When the Lord speaks to a person, is it always crystal clear? Is it always obvious? Is it possible to be uncertain at first?

3. Why do you think it took four tries before Samuel understood that this was God speaking?

Suggested Prayer: "Lord, help me to recognize your presence with me."

SEVENTEEN

Air?

Faith is being . . . certain of what we do not see.
Hebrews 11:1

HAVE YOU EVER tried to explain to a young child what air is? The conversation goes something like this:

"The air sure is fresh tonight!"
"What is 'air' anyway?"
"Well . . . the air is what you breathe."
"I'm not breathing anything!"
"You are too."
"Am not . . . I don't see it."
"Well, it's there. And if it weren't, you would be in big trouble."

The Holy Spirit is invisible. But the Spirit is as real as the air we breathe . . . and as important.

The Holy Spirit is like the fresh air of heaven. The Holy Spirit gives us the life of heaven. The Holy Spirit reveals the Father and the Son to us.

Suggested Prayer: "Father, I open my heart to the presence of your Holy Spirit."

EIGHTEEN

Jesus' Secret

The Spirit of the Lord will rest on him—the Spirit of wisdom and of understanding, the Spirit of counsel and of power, the Spirit of knowledge and of the fear of the Lord. **Isaiah 11:2**

HAVE YOU EVER WONDERED how Jesus did the things he did? How he healed people, how he knew what some of their thoughts were, how he prayed, how he understood what the Father wanted him to do, and how he received the power to do it?

The New Testament gives us the answer: Jesus was "led by the Spirit" (Matthew 4:1).

It's easy to think Jesus was some kind of Superman, someone who had supernatural power which he could turn on and off as he wished.

But the Bible tells us that Jesus relied on the power of the Holy Spirit. He didn't do whatever he wanted to do; he only did what the Father wanted him to do. It was the Spirit who showed him what to do and gave him the power to do it.

Suggested Prayer: "Father, if Jesus had to rely on the Holy Spirit, I know that I do. I want to be filled with the Spirit and led by the Spirit."

NINETEEN

Tickets

I will ask the Father, and he will give you another Counselor to be with you forever—the Spirit of truth.

John 14:16

IMAGINE FOR A MOMENT that you are an avid gymnastics fan. You discover that the Russian Olympic team will compete against the American team at your hometown arena next Friday night.

But there are no more tickets available at the local ticket outlet.

Your older brother says, "Put an advertisement in the newspaper. Maybe someone will sell you their tickets."

Your favorite uncle says, "Forget that. It just so happens that the coach of the American team is my best friend. I'll give him a call and I'm sure he can get some tickets."

Would you go with your older brother's plan or your uncle's plan for getting the tickets?

Your uncle's plan, of course.

Why?

Because your uncle has personal influence. His request will carry more weight than your newspaper advertisement will.

When you ask the Father to give you the Holy Spirit, you have to remember something. You're not the only one asking. Jesus is asking the Father to give you the Holy Spirit too.

How do you think the Father is going to respond to a request like that from his Son?

Suggested Prayer: "Father, hear my prayer, and hear the prayer of your Son Jesus."

TWENTY

The Reluctant Requester

So I say to you: Ask and it will be given to you; seek and you will find; knock and the door will be opened to you. For everyone who asks receives; he who seeks finds; and to him who knocks, the door will be opened. **Luke 11:9-10**

SOMETIMES PEOPLE HESITATE to ask for the Holy Spirit. Why?

- They may think they are not worthy to ask for such a gift.
- They may think they are asking for too much.
- They may be afraid to ask, because they don't want to be disappointed.

Jesus knows about all that. He knows that for all these reasons and many others we can be reluctant to ask.

Let's say you wanted to encourage someone to ask for something. For whatever reason, you knew that this person was shy about asking. But you also knew that he was asking for something very valuable and that if he asked, he would definitely receive.

How would you encourage that person to ask?

You would probably say it as clearly and as strongly as you could say it: "Go ahead, *ask* already!" You would

probably repeat yourself, to emphasize your point.
It does appear that Jesus is trying to do just that.

Suggested Prayer: "Lord Jesus, thank you for making it so clear."

TWENTY-ONE

The Anxious Planter

*What shall we say the kingdom of God is like, or
what parable shall we use to describe it? It is like a
mustard seed, which is the smallest seed you plant in
the ground. Yet when planted, it grows and becomes
the largest of all garden plants, with such big
branches that the birds of the air can perch in its
shade.* **Mark 4:30-32**

THE YOUNG GIRL could hardly believe that the tomato seed in
her hand could become a tomato plant. But she gave it a try
anyway. She put the tomato seed in a plastic cup full of dirt.
Then she watched and waited.

She didn't see much action after ten minutes, so she dug
up the seed to see how it was coming along. Disappointed,
she put the seed back in the dirt.

A few days later, she noticed a small green shoot coming
out of the ground. "No way is this a tomato plant—look how
small it is!" She pulled the green growth out of the dirt and
took it to her mother.

Her mother said, "Don't worry! I've done this hundreds of
times and I know it works. Put the plant back in the ground
and let it grow. Keep it in the sun and give it a little water
each day, but don't pull it out to inspect it."

Being baptized in the Spirit is a beginning. It's like a seed.

Because it is new to us, it is easy to be anxious, like the young girl was anxious about the tomato seed. You may ask yourself: "Was I really baptized in the Spirit?" "Did I really speak in tongues, or was I just making it up?"

Those questions are natural, but focusing on them is like pulling the plant up every morning to see "if it's really working."

Instead, we should just place the pot in the sunlight and give it a little water each day. For us that means taking a short time each day to pray. It means taking opportunities to pray in tongues, even if it is only a little bit, without examining it under a microscope.

Suggested Prayer: "Father, thank you for the gift of the Holy Spirit. Thank you for causing small seeds to grow into large plants that bear much fruit."

TWENTY-TWO

Why Not Today?

I will exalt you, my God the King;
I will praise your name for ever and ever.
Every day I will praise you
and extol your name for ever and ever.

Psalm 145:1-2

HAVE YOU EVER THOUGHT ABOUT what would happen if God turned his back on us, even for a single day? What if . . .

- The sun didn't come up in the morning.
- The air we breathe disappeared for a few short minutes.

Thank God that he is not fickle, up and down, hot and cold. He is steady and faithful, every day.

We are not always as steady as God is. Sometimes we feel like a million bucks, sometimes we feel like a penny on a railroad track, run over by a train.

Whether we feel close to God or far away, we can praise him every day because:

- He's worthy.
- He's watching out for us.
- He's providing for us.
  "Every day I will praise you."

155

Why not today?

Suggested Prayer: Open to one of the "Praise Psalms" at the end of the Book of Psalms (Psalms 145-150). Select one and make it your prayer of praise today.

TWENTY-THREE

Bread to Give Away

*Suppose one of you has a friend, and he goes to him
at midnight and says, "Friend, lend me three loaves of
bread, because a friend of mine on a journey has come
to me, and I have nothing to set before him."*

Luke 11:5-6

JESUS TOLD A STORY about a man who had a surprise visit from
a friend late at night. The man didn't have any food to offer
his friend, so he went to his neighbor and asked for some
bread to give to his friend.

At first, the neighbor wasn't too eager to help. But the man
insisted; he knew that his guest needed some bread!
Because of the man's boldness the neighbor gave him bread,
and the man gave it to his guest.

After the story, Jesus said those words we have been
listening to throughout this course: "Ask and it will be given
to you . . ."

What's the significance of Jesus' words?

The gift of the Holy Spirit is for us. But it is not just for us.
The Holy Spirit gives us the power to love others.

Do you know someone who needs bread from heaven?
Perhaps a neighbor or a relative who doesn't know the love
of Jesus?

Take a moment and pray for that person.

Is there someone at school who could use some extra kindness, some friendship, some love?

Ask God to give you the power of the Holy Spirit to show love to that person today.

Suggested Prayer: "Lord give me what I need to show your love to others."

TWENTY-FOUR

The Crafty Liar

Now the serpent was more crafty than any of the wild animals the Lord God had made. He said to the woman, "Did God really say . . . ?" **Genesis 3:1**

JESUS CALLED THE DEVIL A LIAR, a murderer, and a thief.

What does this passage from the Book of Genesis tell us about the way this liar, murderer, and thief works?

To begin with, he is crafty: shrewd, subtle, tricky, clever, deceitful, not too obvious.

Notice how crafty he was with the woman.

He asked a simple question. "Did God *really* say . . . ?" Sounds like a pretty straightforward, honest question, doesn't it?

Do you think the serpent honestly wondered what God said? Or did he have something else up his sleeve?

What impact did the serpent have on the woman? Did she trust God more or less as a result of listening to the snake?

Suggested Prayer: "Lord Jesus, you came to expose and destroy the works of the devil. Help me to see through his crafty schemes."

TWENTY-FIVE

All Together Now

When the day of Pentecost came, they were all together in one place. **Acts 2:1**

A COLLEGE STUDENT WAS TAKING a course on Life in the Holy Spirit. He was a little skeptical about the gift of the Holy Spirit. But he was also hungry for God.

It was the week before the prayer session. Dan was alone in his apartment. He was sitting on the couch, taking some time to pray.

In the next apartment, he could hear some women's voices. He wasn't sure what they were doing, but it sounded like they were praying.

Dan kept on praying and before he knew it the Holy Spirit was upon him. He began to speak in a language he didn't understand.

The next day, he discovered something interesting. The women next door were praying, all right. They were praying over one another to be baptized in the Holy Spirit.

Something happens when people get together to pray. In the Book of Acts, the Holy Spirit would often fall on a group of people gathered together.

If you want to put a fire out, just scatter the burning logs and the fire will die down. But gather the logs together and the fire grows stronger.

Suggested Prayer: "Lord, thank you for the support and strength that comes through a body of people who are gathered together in your name."

Dan's Story

I HAD NO CONCEPT OF GOD or Christianity, that I can remember, during my first four years of life. My mother—who raised me by herself—found out when I was three years old that indeed, God really did love her, had a wonderful plan for her life, and wanted to relate with her in a personal way. When her faith was renewed, she took me home and prayed for me. While she prayed, God showed her that his hand was on me and that he was taking care of me.

As I grew older, my mother spent many hours teaching me about Jesus and telling me that he loves me. She stressed the importance of a life of prayer and intimacy with my heavenly Father. The older I became, the more I understood my faith, and the more I wanted to be a Christian. As a little boy, however, being a Christian didn't mean much to me, because no matter how hard I tried, I never could satisfy my desire to be closer to God. Also, I did not know how to gain access to God's grace for doing tough things that I knew were right.

I was terribly ashamed of my faith in God and would literally feel sick to my stomach when God was mentioned in my public school. If anyone would ask me if I believed in God, or if I went to church, I would get very nervous and deny Jesus. On the other hand, I would feel the same way when I was reminded that it is our duty as Christians to tell people about Jesus. For years I tried to break free of my fear—or shame—but the only way I knew how to do this was through my awfully weak willpower.

My mother made me go to church, but never forced God on me. She wanted me to choose Jesus on my own. She wanted me to grow in the Lord, but she did not want to make it happen; she knew that if she tried to do that, she would find a way to mess it up—something people are good at doing. Instead of forcing me to choose for God, she evangelized me, she taught me about Christ, she fulfilled her responsibility to train me in the ways of God, and most of all, she spent hours praying that I would take her instruction to heart.

God indeed listened to the prayers of a broken, prayerful mother. By the time I was in eighth grade, God brought me to a place in my heart where I knew that I had to choose for God and that I needed to start my walk with him. While I was at a prayer meeting on a Sunday afternoon, God started to move among the people gathered to pray there. People were being moved by the Spirit of God in a very exciting way. People were crying, laughing, smiling, being delivered, healed, and restored. I wanted what they were having, but I was too ashamed to be seen praying. I was especially afraid that my mother or some other lady might see me praying or being moved by God and smile and say to herself, "Aw, isn't that nice!" I tried to pray when I got home, but as always when I prayed, I couldn't come close to expressing what was in my heart, and I became very frustrated.

Several weeks later, Mr. Mangan, the principal of the Christian school that I was attending, invited us to be baptized in the Holy Spirit. This aroused an interest to hear more. In the course of a few weeks, Mr. Mangan taught us about the Four Spiritual Laws and the Holy Spirit. When the time came for us to ask to be filled with the Spirit, I was eager, as was the rest of the class, to enter into a new relationship with my Father.

The day we were baptized in the Spirit, we spent the entire school day praying, being empowered by God's Spirit, being renewed by his presence, and enjoying the change in our lives. As I was prayed over, I was instantly empowered to communicate with God in a way that expressed what I was moved to pray (tongues). No longer did I feel frustrated when praying to God. Instantly, I was freed from my fear of praying out loud in front of people. For the first time in my life, I experienced God actually saying something to me. Later that day as I was reading my Bible, I had much more insight and understanding about what I was reading. Indeed, God changed me tremendously in just one day!

As I grew closer to God, I was able to do things that I had never done before. One day I was praying over a friend who had a leg that was a bit shorter than the other one. As I prayed I saw the shorter leg grow past the longer leg and then shorten to be perfectly even with it. My friend was healed!

Before this experience, I not only found it hard to talk about God to non-Christians, but I didn't even like talking about God to my Christian friends. But after my eighth-grade year had gone by, I went to a Christian summer camp and on the last day encouraged my friends in the closing ceremony to live to please God first, and then each other. I had done it! I actually called people on to follow Jesus, and I did it in front of about a hundred people. That was no doubt an act of God, because not only was I previously ashamed of

God, but I was very timid and did not like public speaking at all. Now the Holy Spirit has changed me so much that I enjoy speaking in front of large groups of people.

For the next year and a half, God brought me closer to him and used me more to call my friends on to follow him. By the time I was in the public schools again in tenth grade, I was prepared to be among non-Christians and hold on to my faith. I witnessed to several people, overcoming my fear and shame. In fact, the Holy Spirit worked in my heart to the extent that I stood up for Jesus when he or Christians were criticized.

That year I had a speech class, where I had many opportunities to share the gospel in the class. For the final speech we were to talk about what success meant to us. At first, I was going to take the easy way out and talk about worldly success: wealth, fame, power, happiness, etc. But I was convicted by the Holy Spirit to speak the truth, not lies. I decided to speak on success in God's eyes. The speech went very well. Several people told me that they were grateful that I spoke about God. Another person asked me for a script of my speech.

God, through his Spirit, has changed my life. He has shown me how to find success in overcoming fear. He has shown me how to draw near to him. He has shown me how to speak to him when I don't know what to say. Looking back on my short life, I am convinced that something very significant took place that day when I dedicated my life to Jesus and asked to be filled with his Spirit.

Robin's Story

I'M THIRTEEN YEARS OLD and I love to play soccer. (We call it football where I come from.) Some months ago, I was spiked on the ankle, which later developed an infection that wouldn't heal. I even had plastic surgery to replace some skin over the ankle, but that didn't work. It was beginning to look like this might be a long-term problem. In fact, I had to miss about three months of school.

When we realized that nothing was working, my dad and I decided to pray together every day for my ankle. It then began to heal very quickly, much faster than the doctor expected it to. In a few short days it was completely better.

On the Friday evening after this happened, I was home by myself. I began to pray and thank God for healing my ankle and for some reason I can't really explain, I felt like praying more and more.

I felt a strong urge to give my life more completely to the Lord. I had been a Christian, but I wanted to make a stronger commitment to him. Every now and then I used to think about becoming a missionary to some foreign land like Africa. But I couldn't stand to think about it very long because I have this strange fear of snakes. I can't stand them—even to look at them in a zoo is a big challenge for me.

I mention this because I felt like telling Jesus that I would go anywhere he called me to go, even if it meant some place full of snakes.

As I was praying like this—by myself in my bedroom—I began to experience God with me in a powerful way. I surprised myself and started to cry, something that hadn't happened in a long time. It seemed like I couldn't stop, but I didn't really want to anyway, since no one else was around and it was good to be so close to God.

While I was praying like this, I felt like I was in the presence of God in his throne room in heaven. My eyes were closed, but it seemed like he was right there in my room with me. I could see too that the devil was there and very angry— as if he had been holding me back for a while and was mad that I was being filled with the Spirit.

After a couple of hours of this, my dad came home and went up to my room. He could see that something had been going on so he prayed with me. It was like being filled all over again. With my eyes closed, I could see white water bubbling up all around me with a dove in front of the water. It's hard to explain, but I could see it with my eyes closed, as if it were happening right there in the room.

I didn't know it at the time, but that same evening my close friend David was attending a prayer meeting with his family. For the first time he felt God speaking to him so strongly that he thought he should tell the rest of the people at the meeting. This was a pretty gutsy thing for him to do, being only twelve years old at the time. He told everyone that God showed him that the present generation of young people would be great people for the Lord when they grew up. He didn't realize that the Lord was filling me with his Spirit at the same time!

The next day, David had a very similar experience of the

Holy Spirit coming on him. Then it happened to another friend of mine, Allen, on Sunday evening. When the three of us—myself, David, and Allen—talked together, we realized that God was doing something with us. We felt that we should share this with our friends at school (we went to different schools). So we began to tell our friends about being Christians and the love of Jesus for people. We were pretty surprised at how open others were to hearing this. There was some teasing, but not much; mainly they were quite interested.

We decided to start a Bible study at my house on Saturday afternoon. There's no adults leading it, just us. We've had about six friends from school join us. From our telling what has happened with us, two of my friends have become Christians as well as some of David and Allen's friends. David says that this shows you don't have to be a certain age—like twenty-one—for God to work with you.

Erica's Story

WHEN MY DAD APPROACHED ME about being baptized in the Holy Spirit, I said that it was fine with me, though I knew very little about what he meant. I had already given my life to Jesus and wanted to follow him, but, being only seven years old, I didn't know all that being a Christian entailed. Since I was the eldest, my dad figured he would learn how the Lord worked with young people by starting with me. Then he would pray with the rest of the family. He decided to use something called a "Life in the Spirit Seminar" and bring it down to my level.

I was particularly excited when he suggested we invite a couple of my friends to do it also. We would have to speak with their parents but I was hoping that Betsy and Nicole could come. Because my dad wanted to do it in one weekend the girls would be asked to stay overnight. At the time I was more excited about having two of my friends over for the night than I was about anything spiritual.

I distinctly remember being excited when my dad told me that everything was going to work out. I know that none of the three of us knew what we were getting into even though our parents tried to help us understand it some before the sessions started.

On Friday night after dinner my dad took us into his small office in the basement of our house. There he gave us the first two lessons and told us about the Four Spiritual Laws. During the Saturday morning session we shared and prayed and sang and the four of us even wrote a simple song which we called "The Four Spiritual Laws" and recorded it onto a tape so we wouldn't forget it.

In the middle of the afternoon my dad prayed over each of us to renew our commitment to the Lord and to be baptized in the Holy Spirit. I began to speak in tongues as soon as I was prayed over. From what I remember it was like the most natural experience in the world. I did not need to force it at all, and I was not even frightened. It was something that I will never forget. But, being so young, I did not fully comprehend all that took place. It was explained very well, but it took me time to grasp the big thing that took place in my dad's little office.

What helped me most to appreciate and understand the experience were the several times later on when our family went through the seminar again and prayed for the Lord to renew us in the baptism of the Holy Spirit. As I got older I began to see the effect that it had on my life. It changed the way I spoke to God. If I did not know what to say to him, he would always give me the words. My prayer to him now seems to mean more to me because I know that I can say anything to him and he will understand. If we had not prayed for God's renewal after the first experience, I know that for a fact, it would not have meant as much to me as it now does.

As I grew up so did my faith. Each time we went through the seminar as a family I found that I learned something new about myself and the Holy Spirit. I learned how unique it was to be in such a close relationship with Jesus. I feel that I am more willing to converse with him. One of the main things I have found out is that you can never learn too much about the life God has for us in the Holy Spirit.

Maraed's Story

MY NAME IS MARAED, an Irish form of "Mary." My family is Catholic and we live in Belfast, Northern Ireland. When I was about nine years old (a few years ago now) I had a most unexpected experience.

I had been out in my backyard when I looked into what we call a "wendy"—our word for a kind of doghouse. It was a complete mess after I had worked hard to clean it up. It's hard now to remember the exact details, but something like that got me raging with anger. I came storming into the house, complaining to my mother.

We sat down and talked things over and I settled down, feeling much better. Then my mom suggested we pray, and we did. I can remember my mother thanking God that he was with us to help us in our daily lives.

Now I should mention that up until this time, I believed in God—I knew that he existed. But I really didn't think he had much of anything to do with me. I had heard my parents speak of being filled with the Holy Spirit, but I had no idea what that was all about. I was soon to find out.

For some reason, when my mother began to pray with me, I began to cry. I wasn't upset anymore and I was feeling pretty happy, but the tears just came. And they didn't stop.

A few minutes later, I was still crying and the tears were streaming down pretty heavily. I began to pray with words I didn't understand. My mom called it the gift of tongues.

This was all very surprising to me. As best I can remember, I wasn't even asking Jesus to fill me with the Spirit or help me to pray. It just happened.

I noticed a real difference in my understanding of God after that experience. It seems like it was the beginning of something new between me and God. I began to realize that he is really a part of my life and I have a love for him that I didn't know before.

Life in the Spirit
for Your Kids

Life in the Spirit for Your Kids has been a successful tool used around the world to reach young people for Christ in the power of the Holy Spirit.

If you would like information regarding purchasing *Life in the Spirit for Your Kids* write to:

Dave Mangan
3235 Edgewood Drive
Ann Arbor, Michigan 48104

or e-mail to: dmangan@rc.net